Beetle Mania

or, How I Learned to Stop Worrying and Love the Bug

Alessandro Pasi

Beetle Mania

or, How I Learned to Stop Worrying and Love the Bug

Thomas Dunne Books
St. Martin's Press   New York

Acknowledgments

The author expresses sincere gratitude: for her ongoing critique, to Alessandra Puato, a journalist over and above being his companion; for his fastidiousness and extreme competence on the history of the Beetle, to Massimo Tentori, president of the Club Amici del Maggiolino (Friends of the Beetle Club); for her patience in answering the oddest inquiries, to Federica Bennato di Autogerma; for historical images of the Volkswagen, to Dr. Manfred Grieger of the Wolfsburg Historical Museum. Thanks, also, to Vando Pagliardini and Massimo Cattaruzza who endured long nights at work and dozens of phone calls to lay this out book in the best possible way.

THOMAS DUNNE BOOKS
An imprint of St. Martin's Press.

www.stmartins.com

ISBN 0-312-26524-7

First published in Italy by Arnoldo Mondadori S.p.A.

First U.S. Edition.

10 9 8 7 6 5 4 3 2 1

Printed and bound in Spain by Artes Gráficas Toledo, S.A.U.
D.L. TO: 1568-2000

Table of Contents

In the Beginning was the Egg

Imagine for a moment that we could set foot in the century's attic. And that we only had a minute to choose—among thousands of objects—what we would like to hand down to later generations. This product would have to be on the list. Twentieth Century history is its history, too. "It" is the Beetle—that "ugly black bug" as *The New York Times* dubbed it. Yet, all by itself it won its right to immortality. Nowadays its exploits are

Still, the Beetle's story cannot be summarized by technical descriptions of models and modifications, no matter how precise. That would be like trying to comprehend the German History by measuring the disparate length of mustaches on German emperors and Adolf Hitler.

Indeed, even the most patently banal human creation, whether the emblem on a Prussian helmet or the finned head of an engine, always has a

passed along by countless fan clubs from Los Angeles to Moscow. And numerous books, fanzines, and Internet sites deal with the long life of the little German car born in 1938. Even Volkswagen, its mother house, feeds the legend. It has opened the archives and no longer treats the car's Nazi roots with embarrassment but instead promotes inquiry and research into that early stage of its life. So now it is fairly easy to review the genesis and modification of models and versions, chassis numbers, and engine capacity, and the coordination of upholstery and body colors.

larger beginning and a social interpretation that is rich with references and allusions. The Beetle, for example, is air-cooled because that was the best technical solution at the time. But it was only the best because few households had garages and the water used for cooling would freeze in winter.

Volkswagen used the image of an egg in an ad campaign from the early Sixties. The ad's "pay off" or slogan said "Some shapes just can't be improved". Aside from other technical features, the easiest way to distinguish one Beetle from another is a glance at the rear window. The split window typified the 1938–1953 period; the oval window, the years from 1953 to 1957; and the rectangular window, from 1958 on. In 1964, the shape of the license light changed to rectangular and the so-called "Pope's nose" disappeared.

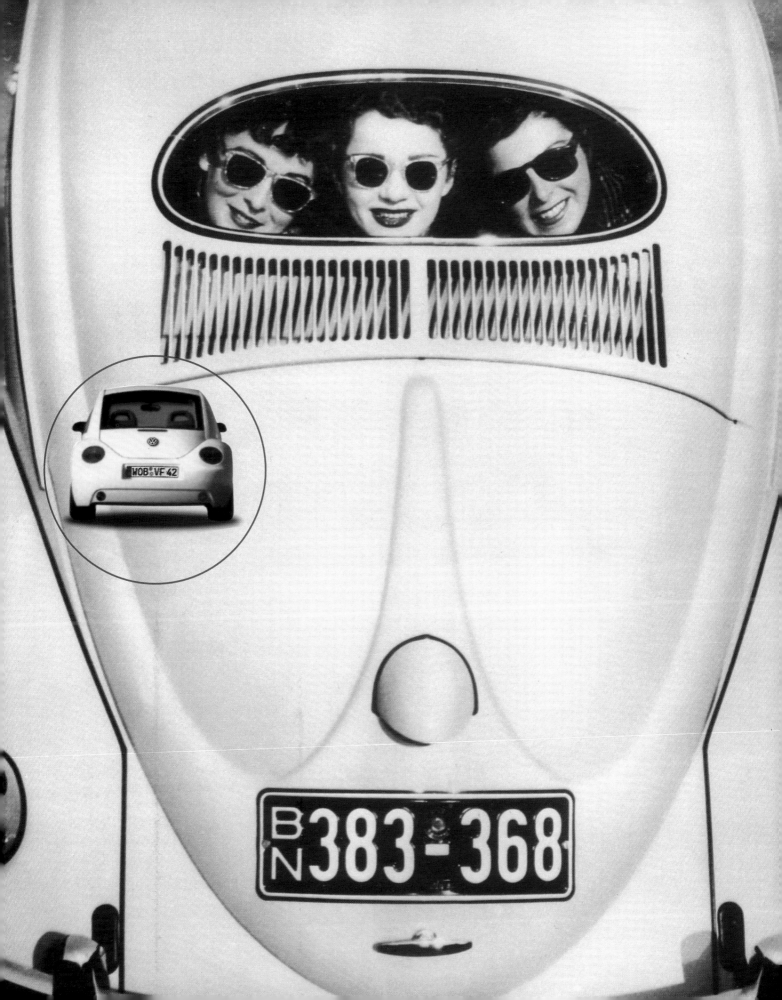

Quest for the Ideal Form

This book aims to tell the story of "Mr. Beetle" wherever that history intersects daily life, peace and war, social cohesion and protest, art and cinema. Starting from its conceptual birth. From its shape. From its origins.

"In the beginning"—as it is said in the Book of books—was the drop of water and man found no greater perfection. Or, if you prefer something more earthy, in the beginning was the egg, the animal world product that most resembles a drop of water and that Volkswagen used for one of its more famous ads. How better to remember that there are things like the Beetle that are already perfect when they are born? The beginning was the year 1928. At that time, one of the most innovative designers of the century (generically labeled architects at the time), was the Swiss citizen Charles-Edouard Le Corbusier. He was fascinated by this new means of transportation and, in thinking about the ideal automobile, took inspiration from that perfect form—the drop of water. In one fell swoop his designs outdated everything that had gone before. Of course cars that looked like carriages had been designed for a long time, but after Corbusier a whole generation of designers would labor to

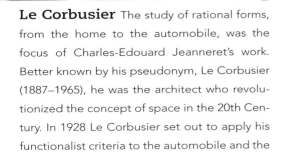

Le Corbusier The study of rational forms, from the home to the automobile, was the focus of Charles-Edouard Jeanneret's work. Better known by his pseudonym, Le Corbusier (1887–1965), he was the architect who revolutionized the concept of space in the 20th Century. In 1928 Le Corbusier set out to apply his functionalist criteria to the automobile and the Maxi was born. It was an extremely aerodynamic vehicle whose development followed the ideal form of a drop of water. Le Corbusier's goal was to secure maximum habitability for its occupants. Thus, rather than occupying the car's nose, its engine was situated in the rear, a solution eventually adopted for the Beetle.

realize the dream of replicating that ideal form for all vehicles, from ships to airplanes.

Among them was a young Bohemian engineer, Ferdinand Porsche, who would soon enter history as the inventor of the Beetle. We do not know how much Porsche knew about the work of Le Corbusier, who saw the home as a machine for living and the automobile as a habitat. It was rotund and functional as a drop of water, and in

Ferdinand Porsche

An engineer with Bohemian roots, Porsche (1875–1951) conceived and created the Beetle between 1934 and 1938. Above, from left, we see the profile of his first prototype (with external headlights and a front hood in two sections), the technical drawing of the definitive model, and finally, the Beetle in profile. We don't know how much Le Corbusier might have influenced Porsche, but the connections between his ideal car (below) and the Beetle are unmistakable.

Left, lateral and three-quarter frontal views of the Maxi, the ideal automobile designed by Le Corbusier. This model was made of wood by the coach maker Giugiaro-Italdesign in the early Eighties and it faithfully follows the Swiss architect's drawings.

it he provided comfort and roominess. We only have to compare the outline of the Volkswagen with Le Corbusier's studies for his ideal car—the 1928 Maxi—to see the striking resemblance.

Nor do we know whether Porsche may have been struck by the soundlessness and weightlessness of the great Graf Zeppelin dirigibles, or by the aircraft-shaped TropfenWagen created by his colleague Edmund Rumpler, or if he may have studied the cars designed by the Czechoslovakian Tatra, a company that was then revolutionizing auto body design. In any case, a very clear line of descent runs between the black-shelled Volkswagen and those uncommon experiments, those innovations in art and technology that made the Thirties so pivotal.

Born in 1938 at the height of the Third Reich with flowing contours, receding fenders, and

TropfenWagen

Literally a "toy car", this vehicle was created by German designer Edmund Rumpler and presented at the Berlin Auto Show of 1921 (now preserved at the Deutsche Museum in Munich). Rumpler, an aeronautical engineer, sought to apply his study of aircraft aerodynamics to an earthbound vehicle in order to reduce forward wind resistance to a minimum. In this sense, the TropfenWagen is one of the Beetle's ancestors.

streamlined headlights, the Beetle came into the world as a child of those ideas—of the shapes of water, spirals, and lightness; of technology; and of the determination to shorten distances, and to astonish the viewer. The Beetle epitomizes the years between the two wars; it concentrates and encapsulates the thinking of that first fragment of the century. And yet, it is also one of the few human products that has been able to slough a similar legacy off its back.

Leica I Designed in 1925, this camera and the Beetle are the only prewar products that have survived to our day. They have one principle in common—technology on a human scale.

Zeppelins no longer streak across the sky and cars are no longer inspired by airplanes, but the Beetle continues to zip around the four corners of the earth.

The fascinating mystery of the Beetle (with its hundred names: Käfer, Beetle, Cox, Fusca, Escarabajo . . .)—how an object born under Nazism could come down to us essentially unchanged—lies in its being simultaneously the product of a lust for power (the regime of Adolf Hitler) and the fruit of an advanced automotive school (Porsche and the Austro-Hungarian engineers).

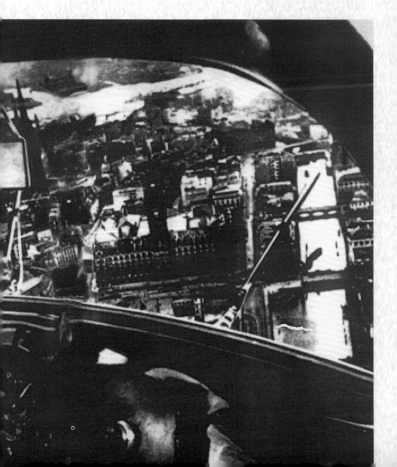

Above, the dirigible Zeppelin L59 in the First World War. The Zeppelin's design concentrated technologies to combine maximal lightness and strength, a principle seen in the cars conceived by Porsche. Left, a Beetle "in flight" (from a Fifties ad).

The answer is that Mr. Beetle has had the good fortune and glory to inherit the dominant traits of the second of these two chromosomal chains, and this explains its immortality. Quite simply, under that steel shell

technology was truly scaled to the humans that the car was born to "serve". And thus, once the war was over, the Beetle, the product of the Führer's will, could return to city streets and country lanes wrapped in an aura of sympathy and the swastika that had waved over its birthplace was forgotten.

Mr. Beetle's history, therefore, is more illustrative of an idea than a well devised object. Only what was strongest in the era that generated the Beetle could outlive that time and change its social significance with generational frequency.

The Nazi regime did not choose the name "Volkswagen" (the people's car) by accident. Created to give every German the prospect of owning a car, "Operation Käfer" was one means among many to secure the acquiescence of the masses. With the war came military versions, and the Beetle became the Kommandeurwagen (the officials' car), the Kübelwagen (the off-road vehicle for Rommel's North African desert

and the Soviet steppes), and the Schwimmwagen (the amphibious car). The end of the war allowed German workers to discover individual mobility; they used it to get to work on time and contribute to their country's economic miracle.

In the Fifties, along with their non-conformist tweed jackets, American intellectuals who disdained the gigantism of mile-long and expensive Buicks, Cadillacs, and Dodges adopted it as their symbol. In the Sixties, flower-children and hippies found in the little, versatile Beetle—

extravagantly painted and individualized—a tool for protesting consumerism (such as the traditional car, wife, and career found in many sit-coms of the day.)

Then came the cinematic celebration. The Beetle was the first automobile to become a star, in Walt Disney's *Herbie* series, and through its roles in numerous films, from Woody Allen's *Sleeper* to Peter Weir's *Truman Show*.

In the Seventies and Eighties, production in Germany had come to an end and the Beetle became a collectible. From California to the Old World, clubs, associations, and fanzines were launched as were whole newspapers dedicated to "old faithful", as the little Volkswagen was called in Germany.

The Nineties finally saw its resurrection. The New Beetle was born on the assembly line in Puebla, Mexico, and within months an overwhelming enthusiasm broke out in the U.S.—enough to make it a cult object.

We enter the life of Mr. Beetle at the very moment of its conception which occurred, discretely, during a meeting at the grand Kaiserhof Hotel, in 1934 in Berlin.

Genesis

Wherein the story is told of an ambitious dictator who admired America; a keen engineer who wanted everyone to have a car; a war that swept away rhetorical delusions and visions; and a car that survived the bombs. Its name was Beetle.

33

A 14

Infancy of a Small Wonder

Before it was completely destroyed by Allied bombs in 1944, the Kaiserhof Hotel in Berlin had been Hitler's headquarters. It was used for receptions and meetings with Nazi party members for several years between his ascent to power in 1933 and the construction of the new Reich Chancellery. In a short and decisive meeting at the Kaiserhof in May of 1934, three men conceived the design for a wholly revolutionary new car that had not yet stumbled upon its real name, the Beetle.

Seated at the table were Adolf Hitler, the new chancellor of the Reich; Jakob Werlin, a Mercedes-Benz dealer in Munich and the Führer's automotive advisor; and Ferdinand Porsche, the most brilliant automotive engineer in Germany (and perhaps Europe).

Herr Professor, as Porsche was usually addressed by his team at the design studio he founded in Stuttgart, had been called by Werlin two days earlier. He was not ignorant of what he would be discussing with Hitler, though no one had dared to tell him. The project on the table would be the second step in a plan to motorize the masses of the Third Reich following construction of a great highway network, the Autobahnen. It would be a model of the car for everyone, the people's car, the Volkswagen.

Porsche himself had sent the Führer a report on January 17th that year, "On Building a German Economy Car," and asked that his design be examined by a commission.

Within fifteen minutes, Hitler had sketched out the fundamentals of the new car. The Führer had definite ideas. The Volkswagen would have to carry four people, the ideal German family of parents and two children. It would consume very little—covering forty miles per gallon; travel easily at sixty miles an hour over long stretches of highway; and have no ignition trouble, especially in cold weather (garages were rare in Germany). Above all, it had to cost less than 1000 marks, or $400 at the 1934 exchange rate.

Porsche considered this last condition nearly impossible. By comparison, his design for NSU

May 1938: Ferdinand Porsche, left, presents the Volkswagen Cabriolet to Adolf Hitler. The car is called the KdF-Wagen, (the Kraft-durch-Freude Wagen or Strength-through-Joy car), named for the leisure organization attached to the new and only labor union, the Nazis' Labor Front. Hitler charged this organization, headed by Robert Ley, at right in the photo, with the task of building Volkswagenwerk, the factory for the people's car. Above right, Hitler's sketch for the Volkswagen and, below, Porsche's first design with two cylinders and two speeds.

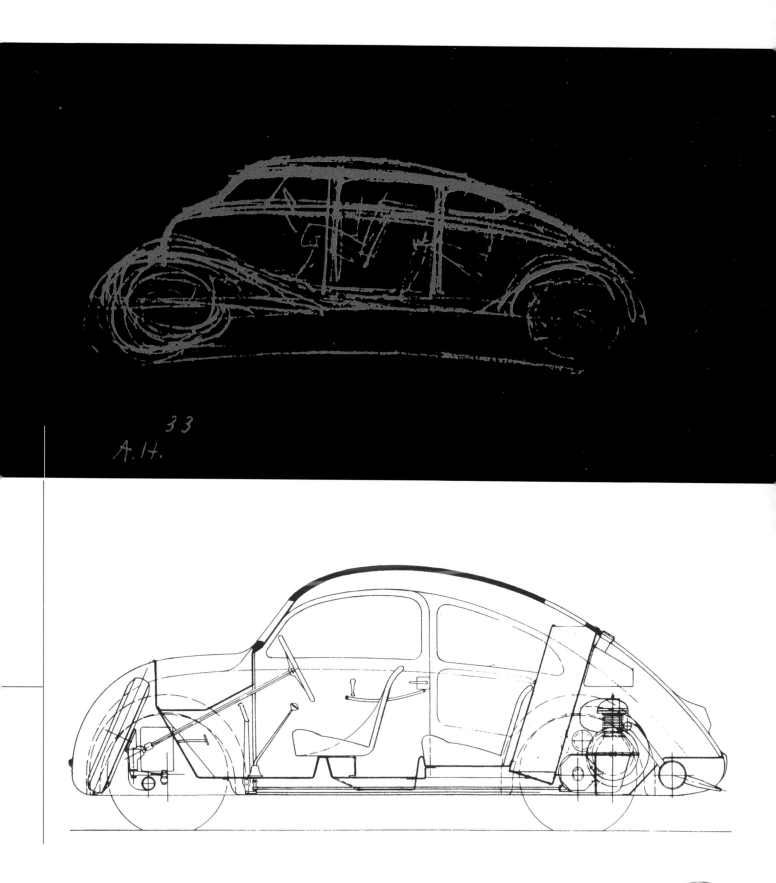

33
A.H.

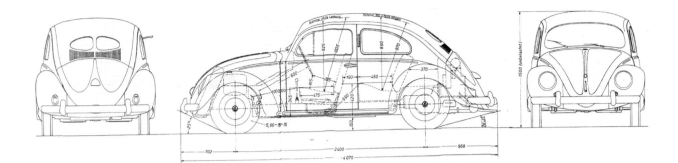

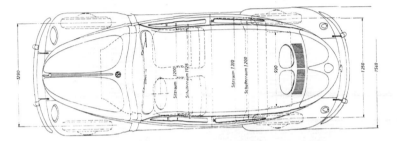

Windkanalmodell 1937
VW 30

had an estimated sales price of 2,000 marks. Germany's smallest car, the Opel Kadet, cost 2,500 marks. In any case, the Führer assured Porsche he would get the financing he needed and that, as Porsche stipulated, the new factory would come equipped with the technology needed to minimize costs. Both men were mindful of Ford's example (and Taylor's methods) in the United States where the revolution in output brought about by the assembly line and piece work permitted millions of Americans to buy Model Ts. Finally, there would be no middle-

men. Unlike other makes, the Volkswagen would only be sold by factory-direct dealers.

In 1989, Porsche's son, Ferry, talked about this proposal in the autobiography he published at age eighty: "In the spring of 1934, Jakob Werlin, a board member at Daimler-Benz AG, arranged a meeting between my father and Hitler. Werlin

himself, who was later named Inspector General for Transportation by Hitler, participated in the meeting. My father explained his plans for the Volkswagen to Hitler, who seemed satisfied with the technical solutions we specified but continued to insist on a price under 1,000 marks. After this important decision, we started work right away, despite the absence of a written contract. The new design became part of the young company's history as the Model (Type) 60."

There are no other witnesses to the meeting, but even in 1985 before Ferry Porsche told his life story, *Automobile Quarterly*, an American magazine specializing in historic cars, published a special edition on the Beetle. It reproduced a series of journal pages with notes and sketches relating to the Kaiserhof meeting. Elske Neidhart, a calligraphy expert at the Deutsches Museum in Munich, certified that the handwriting and automobile sketches were clearly attributable to Adolf Hitler. Only one note at the bottom of one page was dubious, and was probably written by Werlin.

These notes carry enough historical weight to corroborate that it was Hitler's wish to create Germany's largest automobile factory, one that would not compete with existing manufacturers because something completely different was going to be made—"only" a car for the common man.

Even though Hitler's automotive concepts were little more than sketches (he didn't even know how to drive) and a parody of cars that were already in production, from the NSU to the rear-engine Mercedes 150 of 1934, the groundwork for the Volkswagen had been laid. Now

Above left, Ferdinand Porsche shows Hitler a model of the definitive version of the Volkswagen Type 38. Of the three models made at 1:25 scale, the one at left was given to the industrialist Robert Bosch on his 80th birthday, November 23, 1941. In February, 1996 it was appraised at £40,000 ($64,000) for auction at Christie's. Facing page, above, technical drawings for the Volkswagen show its basic measurements and, below, a study of the body shape.

For the first time in his life Porsche faced the prospect of realizing a grand design. The Volkswagen was clearly born under the swastika but the political situation held no apparent interest for Herr Professor. He was a technician—this was his defense when the Allies tried and absolved him at the end of World War II—and to him Hitler was simply the head of government. In any case, fate was placing an unprecedented opportunity in the hands of this mustachioed and no longer young man who had worked under the Hapsburg Empire, the Weimar Republic, and on into the Third Reich unscathed. Let's take a closer look at the nature of this man to whom the Nazis entrusted the most audacious automotive project of the 20th Century.

Porsche had to translate Hitler's ideas into a concrete design and integrate his stipulations.

Ferry Porsche remembered, "Obviously, the Federation of the German Automotive Industry (RDA) was not very enthusiastic when it realized that we had arrived at certain terms. That was entirely understandable because some of the Union's member firms were already producing small cars, and the Model (Type) 60 represented dangerous competition after years of enormous economic hardship. But an agreement was finally reached and, on June 22, 1934, the RDA assigned the Volkswagen to my father with a contract stipulating that, for a monthly compensation of 20,000 marks ($8,000), the vehicle would be ready in ten months."

Above left, Henry Ford and his most famous creation, the Ford Model T, one of the fifteen million units built. Porsche took two trips to the United States, in 1936 and 1937, to study the new manufacturing systems based on the assembly line. Above, two Volkswagen prototypes code-named Type 60 W30. Thirty units were built by Daimler and subjected to severe road tests over more than 30,000 miles. Facing page, a 1939 illustration shows the Volkswagen's gift for climbing; inset, Herbert Kaes, Porsche's nephew and the first Volkswagen test driver.

Peter Koller He was the architect employed by Adolf Hitler to design KdF-Stadt, a new factory town with the Volkswagenwerk at its core to produce the people's car. Koller was a student of Albert Speer (below), the Reich's architect and author of the Nazis' monuments from the Congress of Nuremberg to the Berlin Olympic Stadium and the new Chancellery, Hitler's royal palace. The town site was found after a long aerial reconnaissance in Lower Saxony, in soggy terrain along the Aller River about 90 miles west of Berlin. The area was uninhabited, agricultural and linked to the sea by the Mittelland Canal. KdF-Stadt was envisioned to accommodate more than twelve thousand workers and their families.

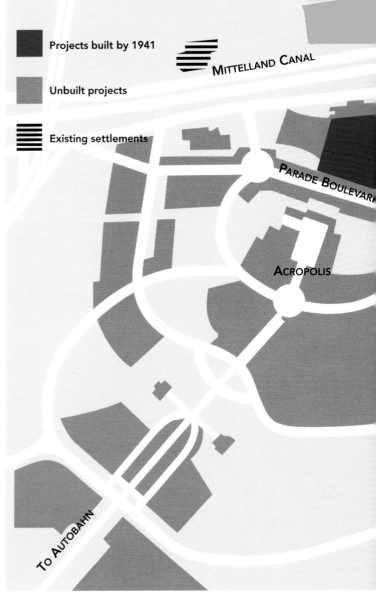

Projects built by 1941

Unbuilt projects

Existing settlements

UNBUILT FACTORY

MITTELLAND CANAL

PARADE BOULEVARD

ACROPOLIS

TO AUTOBAHN

Professor Porsche, I Presume

An engineer with Bohemian roots, Ferdinand Porsche was born September 3, 1875 in Maffersdoerf Neisse. Like Hitler, he was a subject of the Kaiser-König in the Hapsburg monarchy, that Country of KaKlonia (from the German initials for the dual monarchy) ridiculed by Robert Musil. It was an explosive human melting pot ruled by an efficient and rather obtuse aristo-bureaucratic class which could, however, claim historical credit—in the name of moderately progressive politics—for developing rail transportation and an electrical network. Indeed, the young Porsche fell in love with technology when an electric generator was installed in his little town. His first experience with automobiles dated back to 1898 when he started working at Lohner, a small company in Vienna-Florisdorf.

KdF-Stadt

Above, Adolf Hitler at the Volkswagen cornerstone ceremony in Wolfsburg, May 26, 1938. Left, the original urban plan showing segments completed during the first years of World War II. In perfect Nazi style, the plans provided for a small acropolis to dominate a wide boulevard dedicated to pro-Reich demonstrations. Lower left, the Wolfsburg construction site and, in the screened image at right, the commemorative pin for the city's inauguration.

The first car Porsche designed was an electric traction model presented at the Paris Universal Exposition of 1900. Porsche then moved on to Austro-Daimler where he designed the first competition cars (winning a race of considerable import, the Prinz Heinrich Cup, in 1909–1910) and advanced the research and development of military tractors with mixed petroleum-and-electric traction. In 1917, while Adolf Hitler was earning a medal and suffering an eye wound on the French front, Porsche got his engineering degree "honoris causa" from the University of Vienna. Beyond giving him an early interest in technology, growing up under the dual monarchy put Porsche in touch with a small group of engineers, Edmund Rumpler, Hans Ledwinka, and Josef Ganz, who were the boldest and most innovative of the time. Given Eastern Europe's dire road conditions and harsh weather, with appalling winters that froze and silenced engines in the most aristocratic cars, these engineers had detailed a simple but effective concept for the ideal car: light weight and aerodynamic, with an air-cooled engine.

All of Porsche's creations, from the Auto Union competition cars and record-setters to the small-car prototypes for NSU and Zündapp and up to his masterpiece, *der Käfer* (the Beetle), were influenced by the ideas of these Czech and Bohemian engineers. But even if a lot of people pursued similar designs during that period, only one—Porsche—had the determination to see it through. And he did it by adding an abundance of his own

Passenger compartments of the first Volks-wagen and the New Beetle. The dashboard provided a speedometer and radio in the middle with two open cubbyholes on either side. There was no gas gauge; a switch under the dashboard shifted to a reserve tank. The look of the New Beetle's instrumentation evokes that of the Beetle, even if everything is high-tech, like the three-spoked steering wheel.

ideas to what was already in circulation. One glance at the first Beetle prototypes—with the headlights still outside the shell, the divided hood, the grilled but windowless rear end—and then at the definitive versions presented on May 26, 1938, is enough to grasp the immense effort Porsche and his team put into perfecting their design.

One of the first Volkswagens built at Wolfsburg. One feature to note is the total absence of chrome detail-ing; the bumpers (with their famil-iar banana-shaped guards), mold-ings, and hub caps were painted. The mechanical equipment was extremely simple; at right, the engine with its mushroom-shaped filter displaced 984.7 cc, pro-ducing 23.5 horsepower at 3000 revolutions. Engine cooling was air cooled.

1938

The Führer's Support

Hitler guaranteed Porsche the full support of his regime and the German automotive industry or RDA. Members of the organization included Adler, Daimler-Benz, Auto Union, BMW, Man, and the studio of Dr. Engineer Porsche GmbH. The German industrialists quickly figured out that none of their existing factories could pro-

duce the new car in the quantities Hitler wanted, which was at least 10,000 a month. When he observed that the RDA's participation in producing the first prototypes was somewhat forced, Hitler decided, on July 27, 1936 at Koblenz, that Volkswagenwerk would be an independent company under government supervision so that production could start in 1938 at the latest.

Left, a contemporary shot of the Berchtesgaden fire brigade's Volkswagen. Below, the convertible Hitler used at the Berghof, his mountain home in Oberzalzberg, a small town near Berchtesgaden in the heart of the Bavarian Alps. Facing page, the Eagle's Nest at 6,000 feet on Mount Kehlstein. A private road leading to Hitler's residence ends at an elevator dug into the rock and opening inside the refuge.

IIIA·43036

Hitler had a special fascination with what the United States had accomplished, and not only with its cars. He wanted the Germany of the new social pact, defined by the Wagnerian belief in *Blut und Boden* (Blood and Earth), to outdo the democracy of the stars and stripes. The gap would clearly be tough to close. Even if the German worker could scrape together 990 marks, or $360, to buy a Volkswagen (and Hitler invented the savings-book system to help), the operating costs would have been prohibitive. For example, with three man-hours the German worker could purchase three liters of gas (8/10 of a gallon) while for the same amount of work his American counterpart could buy thirty liters (almost eight gallons). A weekend spent driving about three hundred kilometers (186 miles) would cost the German worker one fifth of his weekly wages just for gas.

In 1937 Hitler was persuaded beyond doubt that Volkswagen had to be a National Socialist factory and would have to be created from scratch. His decision solidified at the new Berlin Automotive Exposition. While visiting the Show, the Führer stopped by Opel's display, red in the face. The manufacturer (owned by the American General Motors) was presenting its glossy, resplendent new P4, a fairly small car, for sale at 1450 marks. The old industrialist, Wilhelm von Opel, committed two gaffes in a row. He

Facing page, 1939 advertising pamphlet for the KdF-Wagen. It emphasized the car's practicality (even a woman can change a tire!) and stamina. The man rapping his knuckles on the hood exclaims, "This is steel!". Below, the savings book. Every week a German worker could buy a stamp costing four or five marks until he had saved 990 marks, the price of the car. Below, the propaganda bus for the layaway plan.

greeted Hitler by calling him Herr Hitler (instead of Mein Führer) and, when showing him the Opel P4 he added, "This is our Volkswagen." Hitler spun on his heels without a word. Four days later, Jakob Werlin was called to the Chancellery, soon followed by Robert Ley, who headed the DAF or Deutsche Arbeitsfront (German Labor Front), which was the Nazi labor union.

Hitler told Ley that he had to set up an auto factory, and the "Corporation for the Preparation of the Volkswagen" was quickly established. Ferdinand Porsche, Robert Ley, and his assistant, Bodo Lafferentz, were named to executive posts.

Meanwhile, using the best materials, Daimler-Benz had the

thirty prototypes ready to go (at an apparent cost of 8,000 marks, or $3,200 each). Porsche's son Ferry was charged with coordinating new road tests. The Wehrmacht supplied the two hundred test drivers needed, and a headquarters for the great automotive maneuvers was installed in a barracks at Kornwestheim. In the summer of 1937, the biggest test drive in the history of four wheels took off. Every car had to cover 50,000 kilometers (31,000 miles) without stopping, along a route that incorporated all conceivable driving conditions major highways to alpine passes. The drivers had

"THE FÜHRER'S WILL HAS GIVEN THE PEOPLE THE BEST TECHNOLOGY THAT THE GERMAN CREATIVE SPIRIT CAN PRODUCE"

To keep its price down, the Beetle had to be sold directly by company concessionaires without middlemen. The advertising that launched the new car was especially well composed. These images depict one of the first brochures whose transparent pages revealed additional details of the car as the pages were turned. The images ranged from the bare chassis up to the complete auto body and vice versa. The engine was mounted in the rear, behind the axle, a solution that gave the occupants more room and allowed better access to the engine. The engine could be replaced in little more than an hour.

The sixty years between the Beetle and the New Beetle, launched in 1998, did not pass in vain. The New Beetle is the old one's exact technological and philosophical reverse: produced in limited numbers, front-mounted engine and traction, liquid cooling, the speed and trim of a sports car, luxury finishes, and excellent noise suppression.

to push the engines and torture the machinery by driving like the most mediocre motorists. In total, the thirty cars would have to cover 2,400,000 kilometers, or about 1.5 million miles. The costs soared sky-high but this time it was the DAF's turn to pay. It has been calculated that 30 million marks ($12 million) were invested in the Volkswagen, or about 1,700,000 in today's dollars, but the comparison is flawed because today's auto manufacturers control far greater financial resources.

The Beetle was explicitly conceived to mobilize the typical German family of the Thirties. Thus, with a certain optimism, the sales brochure showed how five people, parents and three children, could travel comfortably together with an array of baggage. In reality, the nose compartment held only two soft-sided bags due to the configuration of the gas tank (modified in the Fifties and Sixties). The car cruised easily at sixty mph and had a range of 250 miles. Every component of the vehicle, by order of Hitler, was made in Germany.

The automotive industry's most tangible progress has been in the field of safety. Volkswagen built the New Beetle according to strict U.S. regulations. Beyond the crush-resistant shell and other features, the New Beetle can absorb collisions up to five mph without damage. It has airbags and anti-intrusion beams in the side doors.

Adolf Hitler could finally celebrate victory at the 1938 Auto Show. "It has taken four years, little by little and with continual modifications, to finish a car for the people." Volkswagenwerk, he said, would have to produce between 400,000 and 500,000 cars a year with a labor force of

For the first time ever, a car's contour was studied in a wind tunnel and this is how the Volkswagen got the aerodynamic lines that were far superior to its competitors. An engineer named Komenda was in charge of developing the body and used a prototype with covered wheels at the Stuttgart Polytechnic to measure a Cx of 0.36, the "drag" coefficient that indicates wind resistance. Very few cars measured as low as 0.40; the Lancia Aprilia had a Cx of 0.47. Moving from the prototype to the production car, the Beetle's Cx rose to 0.41 because of its bumpers. Below, another brochure from 1938 exaggerates the car's dimensions. Note the child's toy cannon.

Der KdF Wagen

Der Innenleuter

Left, the vehicle prepared by Porsche, using the Beetle's engine and drive-train for the September 1939 Berlin-Rome road race. The outbreak of World War II canceled the competition. The Type 64 car had 40 horse-power and could reach a maximum speed of eight-seven mph thanks to its exceptionally aerodynamic lines.

Below, a coin bank from the Forties. The center dial shows the number of marks and pfennigs saved. Facing page, Volkswagens on a propaganda tour of Berlin.

10,000 workers in the first shift and 7,500 in the second. Hitler was convinced that the mechanization of production would produce miracles. In reality, his calculations were pure propaganda. When Volkswagen was finally capable of producing that many Beetles, in 1954, the necessary workforce was more than double the Führer's estimate, or 40,000 employees inclusive of labor and management.

In the meantime, Ley directed Bodo Lafferentz to find the best site for the Volkswagen plant. Lafferentz, who planned activities for the KdF (*Kraft durch Freude* or Strength through Joy), the Labor Front's leisure-time organization, got in a plane and began to patrol Germany at low altitude. He found what he was looking for on the banks of the Mittelland Canal. It was a vast asparagus field owned by Count von der Schulenberg, who lived in the renaissance castle of

Wolfsburg. It lay near the small town of Fallersleben along the Berlin-Hanover road in Lower Saxony. To soothe the Count, who was plainly opposed to watching a factory go up outside the manor windows, Lafferentz lied shamelessly, guaranteeing that the factory would occupy no more than three thousand acres when the plan called for nearly ten thousand. The Count and many farmers in the area had the better part of their land expropriated. Despite Lafferentz's determination, inspections and talks were protracted, lasting until January of 1938.

The Air Force General Staff, to take just one example, maintained that the site was very dangerous because the factory would be altogether too easily targeted in an air attack and, given their proximity, bombs would strike the factory, canal, and railroad. The Count and Countess of Schulenberg moved temporarily to the Hotel Eden in Berlin to try to block construction, but in vain. Reclamation work on the site began, and construction got under way.

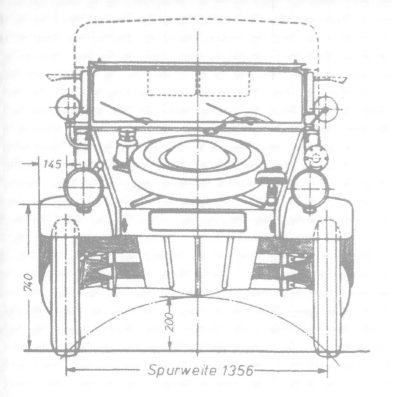

Zugehörige Zeichnugen:

Fahrgestell..........................82.00.01
Ausführungsbestimmungen für Fahrg.......SK 3930
Elektrische Anlage.................820.140.040

Winds of War Over Wolfsburg

An architect named Peter Koller was working with Lafferentz. Born in Styria in 1907, he had won a competition for the reconstruction of Zagreb and as a result met Albert Speer, the architect who was designing Nazism's most important buildings for Hitler, including the new Chancellery.

Koller gladly accepted the chance to build a new city around the Volkswagen factory. It was the first time that a production facility would rise simultaneously with the city for its workers.

Koller was only supposed to concern himself with the city, however, and his urban utopia was a "machine for living." The buildings were all brick in accordance with the functionalist style that was still in vogue in Germany and favored by Hitler. They were to be developed in a U shape whose outer facades nestled against the state highway,

Above, a technical drawing for the combat Volkswagen or Type 82 that was nicknamed the Kübelwagen (Kübel means "bucket" or "tub"; thus, the "bucket car"). Right, the assembly line at Wolfsburg. Facing page, the German Labor Front newspaper spotlights continuity between the Beetle project and the Kübelwagen at war, shown here in Sicily. About 55,000 Kübelwagens were assembled in the Wolfsburg factory between 1940 and 1945.

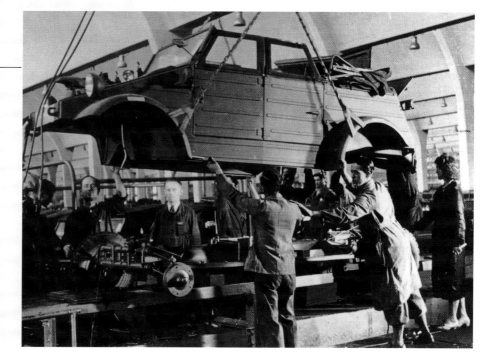

the canal, the railroad, and the front of the factory, which was itself 1.5 kilometers (0.9 miles) long. North of the dwellings, there was to be a monumental road one hundred meters (325 feet) wide. It would be the parade boulevard, in perfect Nazi style, and was in turn dominated by a neoclassical acropolis. From this site on the hill, the Nazi Party's most important buildings—the theaters, the palace of culture, and the concert hall—would slope down to the boulevard.

On the day of the Ascension, May 26, 1938, under sunny skies at Wolfsburg, Hitler laid the cornerstone for the new factory in front of three Beetles, a black sedan, and two black convertibles, one with a dark gray folding top.

The *Hanoverschen Anzeiger*, the local paper, greeted Volkswagen's birth in its pages: "A small world is being created here. A cyclops' fist has landed on the tranquillity of this luminous landscape in Lower Saxony. But it is a modern cyclops who, precisely because he is modern, understands the beauty of labor. . . . One looks from the ceremonial plaza out over the canal and

beyond to a gentle line of forested hills. That is where the most modern and beautiful workers' city in all of Germany will rise. Happy the people who find their homes here."

On the initiative of Benito Mussolini, who was anxious to show Hitler the quality of Italian workmanship, a group of about eight hundred Italian bricklayers showed up and was lodged in a reddish-brown barracks. The 4,400 foot long front wall of the factory was started. Curiously, the factory's foundations were reinforced concrete with no cellar space. Thus the industrial components were located on the ground floor with assembly divisions on the upper floors. But the work proceeded slowly. Germany was re-arming; materials were rationed, and priority had shifted to the military.

On July 20, 1938 construction of the fortified Siegfried Line started along the French border, and all of the building trades were put to work on it. Construction dragged on at Wolfsburg through December 1941 when the needs of the war economy put an end to the new "City of

Strength through Joy," or Stadt der Kraft durch Freude, the KdF-Stadt.

But if the Volkswagen plant was beset by difficulties, conversion of the Beetle to war ends was moving in quick step. By the end of 1939 it was all out war, and while Lafferentz kept the Germans dreaming by showing off the few completed Beetles that were already on the streets of Germany's main cities, Hitler invited Porsche to create an open military vehicle based on the Volkswagen. The Kübelwagen, literally a tub on wheels, was born. The engine—after a first series using the Beetle's 985 cc, 23.5 horsepower model—was upgraded to 1130 cc and 25 horsepower.

Herr Kaefer Goes to War

When Volkswagen was finally operational in 1940, it started by producing military vehicles.

> "THE KÜBEL CAN DO EVERYTHING OUR JEEP DOES ON HALF THE GASOLINE"
> SUPREME ALLIED COMMAND, 1945

Fifty-five thousand Kübelwagens and Kommandeurwagens (a sedan for officers that was a military version of the Beetle) and fifteen thousand Schwimmwagens, the amphibious model, had been built by 1945. Hitler asked Porsche to devise a vehicle that could carry four soldiers and a heavy machine gun, giving rise to the Type 62; the Beetle's designation was Type 60. The platform for both cars was the same. Its mechanical differences were in the drive train (reduction gears were fitted to the rear hubs to augment traction on difficult terrain), the differential (a limited-slip model by ZF was chosen), the air filter (modified so it could "breathe" in the desert), and its ground clearance (a modified suspension system lifted it to 11½ inches compared to 6 inches in the civil version). Its shell was designed to be manufactured with the least possible refine-

Facing page, Field Marshall Erwin Rommel (1891–1944) during the North African Campaign in 1942. The German general deployed a great number of Kübelwagens, which proved indifferent to the heat and sandstorms. Above, a few details of the military vehicle: left, the external spare tire (there was no trunk); center, the dashboard with speedometer and ammeter; above right, the engine was augmented to 1,131 cc to guarantee the army its required minimum of 25 horsepower. Note the air intake hose rising to the left to draw air from an area protected from wind and sand; the jack was secured to the left of the engine. Finally, above, the fuel inlet pipe on the right side of the front hood; a security chain kept the lid from falling off.

ment, using vertical panels and squared-off lines. Because it sat high off the ground, the rear chassis was encased in a slanting, sealed panel. The spare tire and gas inlet were external, while the engine compartment was closed with a metal hatch. The body was open and a light canvas top protected the soldiers in case of bad weather and severe cold, though it was often unavailable. Steven Spielberg's Holocaust film, *Schindler's List*, is very accurate when it shows commander Amön Goeth arriving to take over management of the Nazi death camp. He complains about being driven in an open Kübelwagen at the height of the harsh Polish winter.

Ferry Porsche recalled in his autobiography that, "Before 1940 our plans never included an off-road vehicle. The light and maneuverable Volkswagen had obviously encouraged experimentation, and once led us to mount two tempo- rary folding chairs on a Volkswagen chassis and try it out off-road. The tests were often improvised, but we were more and more amazed by the Volkswagen's versatility. Progressing from the sedan to the off-road vehicle, therefore, was not

The Schwimmwagen was the most original World War II design for an amphibious military vehicle. Starting with the Beetle's chassis and mechanical equipment, Ferdinand Porsche created an extremely useful transport (Type 166/15), which could climb over any obstacle and wade through rivers and other bodies of water. The Schwimmwagen, seen here climbing out of the canal in front of the Wolfsburg factory, had four-wheel drive and a large propeller which engaged the crankshaft by dog clutch when lowered, permitting navigation. The exhaust pipes were mounted above, behind the rear seats, and the front wheels acted as rudders. More than 16,000 were built between 1942 and 1945.

picion was demonstrated by subjecting our VW-Kübel, as the soldiers came to call it, to far more severe tests than the competitors' vehicles."

Porsche's vehicle, initially opposed by top officials of the Oberkomando der Wehrmacht, was put into production on Hitler's order. But Hitler's resolve was not really necessary to demonstrate the advantages of the Volkswagen's military version. German soldiers on every front of the war preferred the Kübelwagen. It was lightweight and robust, it did not require many repairs, and its equipment could deliver it from the worst situations without needing another vehicle to pull it out of the mud. The military Volkswagen displayed equally superb capabilities from the Russian campaign to the African desert. The German army requisitioned several versions of the Kübelwagen including a four-seater with machine gun, a three-seater with

exceptional and was even predictable once the war broke out. The agency responsible for the army's technical equipment at the time was the armaments office and that was where we had to consign our off-road Volkswagen for testing. We were not at all worried about the vehicle's technical readiness and performance in these tests. At least that's what we were thinking, but we were wrong. . . . In the event, their sus-

a radio set, and a two-seater ambulance configuration. The Kübelwagen was light (sixteen hundred pounds), went fifty mph with a range of 275 miles, and gas consumption was about twenty-five miles per gallon, half that of an American jeep.

To train armored troops, a Panzer-Attrappen (Type 823) was also built (with a mock turret and cannon) to acquaint new drivers with maneuvers inside a Panzer without using the real tanks. The Third Reich had an urgent need to conserve materials as it continued to lose territories, and the mineral and energy resources that went with them.

Erwin Rommel, commander of the Afrika Korps, was the most enthusiastic among Germany's top officers about the Kübelwagen. He liked to say that it was the only vehicle that could go anywhere a camel could go. Rommel

had reached Cyrenaica in 1941 to help Italian forces withstand the British advance and drive the British from Egypt, if possible. The Panzer-Attrappen proved extremely effective as a decoy. Rommel had a great number of them delivered (while waiting for the real tanks) and put them on desert maneuvers with bundles of wood tied to the rear end in order to raise huge clouds of dust. British air reconnaissance believed that Rommel's Panzers were already in action and British headquarters delayed the planned offensive to wait for reinforcements. But before the British Matildas arrived, Rommel put his German Panzers on the offensive, surprising the enemy and pushing them back to the Egyptian border, using only three armored divisions. And a lot of Kübelwagens. During Operation Barbarossa, the invasion of the USSR, military Volkswagens were distinguished by their

Facing page, North African Campaign, 1942. A Kübelwagen passes the ruins of a British depot with a sign warning people to stay away. Below, two other military versions of the Beetle. At left, the Kommandeurwagen Type 87E, of which fifty or fewer units were built, equipped with the same mechanical components as the amphibious version including four-wheel drive. At the end of the war, the gas shortage pressured German engineers to find "alternative" fuels; at right, a Kübelwagen with a coal burner under the front hood that produced flammable gas.

easy transit through the mud and snow of the winter of 1941, one of the most unyielding in Russian history. The Volkswagen's air-cooled engine was the only one that started up at more than forty degrees below zero; all it took was a little flame under the starter.

Himmler's SS also made wide use of the Kübelwagen until the Ardennes offensive in the winter of 1944. Then the collapse of the Reich and the shortage of gasoline and spare parts paralyzed them, and the Volkswagens mostly ended up destroyed by air raids, or seized by the Allies.

The conversion of Volkswagenwerk to military production was completed when it started making parts for Junker 88 airplanes and the flying V1 bomb. At that point, the Wolfsburg facility could no longer hope to escape the Allied bombardments that grew more intense from 1943 on.

On the night of April 8, 1943, three waves of bombers dropped thousands of incendiary bombs on Kdf-Stadt, destroying the assembly lines and hitting the prisoners' barracks as well. A British plane struck by anti-aircraft fire crashed into a factory building and destroyed it. The fire lasted three weeks.

According to Ferry Porsche, "from the moment that Wolfsburg became a dense industrial complex, it was a highly recognizable object in air reconnaissance photographs. Plants that had been built expressly for wartime production were divided into smaller pavilions and distributed across a larger area. Moreover, they were usually surrounded by trees and, once camouflaged, were far harder to make out than a factory like Wolfsburg which seemed to be offered up on a platter."

On June 20th and July 5th of 1944 the Allies

 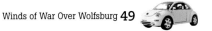

 50 Genesis

carried out two more aerial attacks on Wolfsburg. Ninety bombers escorted by thirty fighters dropped another five hundred bombs in the first wave. Twenty-seven workers died and another hundred were gravely wounded. On July 5th, another wave of bombers and more than three hundred bombs completed destruction of the factory buildings. Following severe damage, many manufacturing processes were removed from the central structures and some were even shifted into underground workshops.

On April 17, 1945, the 102nd American Infantry Division occupied Fallersleben. A little while later Britain's 52nd Division replaced the American forces, and on May 25th Kdf-Stadt was officially renamed Wolfsburg; a few thousand factory workers and about eleven thousand prisoners, mostly Slavs, were left.

Anton Piëch, Porsche's son-in-law and chief executive of Volkswagenwerk, delivered what was left of the factory to two English officers, Colonel Charles Radclyffe and Major Ivan Hirst.

Wolfsburg bombarded. On the night of April 8, 1943, three waves of Allied planes destroyed the assembly lines and zeroed in on the halls and barracks that housed workers and prisoners of war. The factory was hit two more times, on the 20th of June and the 5th of July, 1944. Sixty percent of the Volkswagen factory was in ruins. Nevertheless, 2,030 military vehicles were assembled in the first four months of 1945.

2.

A Happy Adolescence

THIS CAR HAS NO FUTURE, CHORUSED THE BRITISH AND THE AMER-
ICANS; IT'S NOTHING MORE THAN A NAZI RELIC. BUT INSTEAD THE
HOMELY BLACK BUG CONQUERED GERMANY AND THE UNITED
STATES, TOO. HOW COULD IT HAPPEN? SOME WHO LEFT THE AUTO
INDUSTRY ARE STILL WONDERING.

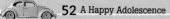

Rebirth:
Mr. Beetle Lands in America

October, 1946: The temperature had already sunk beneath historic lows. But one glance at the sky was enough for him. "*Schnee, es kommt schnee*, sorry, Major, I meant to say that it's going to snow. . . ." A refugee from the eastern front, he was the private gardener to Major Ivan Hirst, the new commander of KdF-Stadt in the British Zone. He already knew it would be a winter to remember.

And sure enough, the first icy waves erupted from the northwest in November. They buried Berlin and dumped a half yard of snow and ice on the plant at Wolfsburg, about ninety miles from the former capital of the Reich. The end of that first bomb-free year was showing signs of a

Ivan Hirst Born in 1916, he arrived at Wolfsburg in August 1945 with the rank of Major. He commanded a unit of the REME, the Royal Electrical and Mechanical Engineers, whose assignment was to recover mechanical equipment and repair electrical systems. He and Colonel Charles Radclyffe were put in charge of Volkswagen. Despite their superiors' scepticism, the two restored production and found a German to whom they could entrust factory management, H.H. Nordhoff. Hirst left Volkswagen in September of 1949.

winter worse than the year before, when the Germans' first months of freedom from Hitler were bitterly cold.

Major Hirst's gardener considered himself a fortunate man. The English officer let him occupy a room in the command villa where water and heat were a sure thing. Miraculously, the factory's heating plant still worked.

The Volkswagenwerk's presses—vast structures more than ten feet tall—had escaped the American aerial bombardments that destroyed the hall roofs and killed twenty-seven workers, but they were now covered only by canvases held up by posts. With the thermometer holding firm under 50 degrees, their lubricating oils and hydraulic fluid would freeze in the first attempt to put the gigantic pressure pumps back in operation.

The Käfer—or Beetle, as the whole world would come to call that German car—factory was completely shut down for nearly two months. As recently as October, Major Hirst and the workers had celebrated a small production record in those conditions. A black car reached the end of the assembly line with a big poster on it that stated ironically, "*10,000 Wagen, und nicht in Magen*" (10,000 cars and nothing in our bellies). In the end, Major Hirst's gardener was not all that lucky, either. He was killed a few days later when he tried to thwart a thief scavenging for beans and potatoes from his garden.

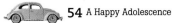

Left, Major Ivan Hirst steps into a Beetle at Wolfsburg in 1945. The Volkswagen factory had been renamed Wolfsburg Motor Works by the British who occupied it. Production started slowly; 138 Kübelwagens were assembled in June of that year and 235 in July. Altogether in 1945, 703 Type 51s were produced, which is to say the Beetle, but on a military version of the chassis that rode higher off the ground. Below, Winston Churchill; a British technical commission examined the Beetle and deemed it technologically outmoded and "too odd".

Mr. Beetle, the Reich's small car for the average driver, was thus reborn. And this second birth at the end of the war was the good one, even if conditions were far more difficult. The factory buildings had suffered significant damage and there were few skilled workers, but in recompense, the small town was filling up

certain body parts that had been produced in Ambi-Budd's Berlin factory, now occupied by the Red Army, had to be made from scratch. But the mechanical equipment—lathes, cutters, etc.—had been saved because workers had scattered them after the first bombardments and hidden them in the countryside or underground. Finally, by a stroke of good fortune, the power plant had suffered minimal harm. A bomb broke through the roof and lodged without exploding between the two main turbines. Had it detonated, the factory would have taken a mortal blow, according to the British. Beyond all this, everything was lacking. There was no food,

with refugees from the German territories now in Soviet hands. The halls were charred, the warehouses were practically empty and, what's more,

and workers were forced to wear Wehrmacht uniforms (without medals) inside the Volkswagen factory and out. They were the only available clothes.

But although the factory was in good enough shape to start production again, it would take human intercession to set the presses in motion. First and fundamental was the determination of Ivan Hirst, who wagered—against the opinion of his superior officers—that the Beetle was not a project for the archives and that the Wolfsburg Motor Works (as the Volkswagen plant was soon rechristened) could resume production and contribute to the new Germany's economic revival.

Facing page, above, a train loaded with Beetles approaches the border in 1946, probably destined for the French armed forces. Below, life starts over in Germany's Year Zero at the end of the Second World War. Above left, a ceremony organized for the one thousandth automobile assembled at Wolfsburg, in March of 1946. At right, in October of the same year, ironic placards greeted the birth of the ten thousandth Beetle: "Better-tasting food and more of it, or we will remember. 10,000 cars and nothing in our bellies."

The second factor was the rapid deterioration of political relations among the powers that had won World War II (the USSR, the U.S., Great Britain, and France). The Allies, especially the British, were plainly worried that persistent harsh living conditions in western Germany would advance the spread of socialist and soviet ideas, creating a potentially subversive climate. Nonetheless, it was the British who realized that they could not bring about the reconstruction of Germany, and this was the third factor driving the rebirth of Wolfsburg. It was essential that the Germans roll up their sleeves and that every industry capable of production resume work as quickly as possible. And The Allies' idea of making the new Germany an exclusively agricultural nation—a kind of European granary where most industrial activity would be eradicated and transferred to the victor countries—was soon abandoned. The English got a press working, organized a work crew, and assembled a pair of cars that were delivered to the British headquarters, which was so bereft of vehicles that another order was immediately placed through Colonel Charles Radclyffe. The parts supply was exhausted, however, and Hirst could only produce eleven Kübelwagens in September. Only one was built in December and the manufacture of Kübelwagens ceased entirely by February 1946.

But Hirst had not set out to produce military vehicles alone. In 1945 he succeeded in manufacturing 703 Type 51s—that is, the Beetle on a military chassis—and a thousand other derivative vehicles for every conceivable use from postal delivery to fire trucks and ambulances. Fifty-eight traditional Beetles were also assembled that year, most of them in December. These vehicles were built with limited supplies and their passenger compartments were extremely frugal. The seats were padded with horsehair and upholstered in cotton. The engine was the 1131 cc (75 x 64 mm) military model. With no sound-absorbing walls in the engine compartment, the boxer engine was unbearably loud. In 1945, a technical commission of the British Society of Motor Manufacturers and Traders arrived in Wolfsburg for a visit guided by Colonel William Rootes. These experts produced a report entitled *Investigation of the Developments in the German Automobile During the Post War Period*. Published in

"THE BEETLE WAS VERY MODERN. ALL WE HAD TO DO WAS MAKE IT BETTER." HEINRICH NORDHOFF, 1948

Below, Heinrich Heinz Nordhoff (in a photo montage showing him in front of an army of workers at Wolfsburg) took charge of the Volkswagen plant January 1st, 1948 and directed it until his death, April 12th, 1968. Within ten years Nordhoff had driven output to more than half a million Beetles a year. In 1968, it hit one million units a year. At right, an advertising poster reads "Yesterday's dream . . . today's reality". Facing page, ad images from the Fifties with "Bon Voyage in the New Year" (on the left).

1946 under the title *Investigation into Design and Performance of the Volkswagen or German People's Car*, the report compared the Beetle to a British car, the 1,185 cc, 30 horsepower Hillman Minx MkIII that had been manufactured with a rear engine since 1932. The car was developed with a conventional chassis, weighed about 1,670 pounds, had a three-speed gearbox, and leaf-spring suspension. In 1940 had it been completely redesigned, with a more modern chassis, more power (35 horses), a four-speed transmission, and more Americanized lines.

The verdict totally favored the British car. The Beetle was pronounced ugly, awkward, noisy

LIMOUSINE

STANDARD- UND EXPORT-MODELL

Until February of 1953, the Beetle was made with a split rear window, one of the chief characteristics—together with side running boards—of Thirties-era cars. From 1949 on, the engine had a new Solex carburetor and, from 1950, a prominent cylindrical air filter. Its engine capacity was 1131 cc and 25 horsepower. A folding canvas sunroof was optional. At left, a Fifties poster shows cars a little sleeker than they really were.

and, in the end, just too odd. It appears that Winston Churchill himself may have settled the Volkswagen affair by making the last words of the technical report: "This car? No future . . ."

In February of 1947 and again in 1948, both Ford and the Australians stepped up for a look. The latter shared the British commission's opinion that the car was antiquated and ungainly. Ford soon abandoned any interest in it as well. Ernest Breech, a spokesman for the American

For the British, there was only one road left to take and it was practically imperative. The factory had to be restored to the Germans. But how? Its owner, so to speak, had been the KdF, the Nazi Labor Front, now declared illegal. All the executives were Nazis and had been dis-

company, released the following to the press, "I think that what we have been offered is not worth a damn". Ford's true motivation was political. Henry Ford II believed that investing in Volkswagen was too risky because the factory was too close to the Soviet line. In essence, Wolfsburg was seen as a site at risk.

missed. Ferdinand Porsche, his son Ferry, and his son-in-law Anton Piëch had been arrested and then freed, but it was clearly inappropriate to reappoint them to a conspicuous role.

The split-window Beetle had semaphore turn indicators (at left) with a
central control on the dashboard.
It was button-operated once the
ignition was on. The passenger
light was over the rear window. The
Export model had a more refined
interior; it even had arm-rest cush-
ions for the rear seats. A door was
fitted to the glove compartment in
1952. The flower vase was an
accessory mounted on many vehicles in those days. Below left, there
was only a single bulb in the tail
light; the brake light was over the
license plate.

A Miracle Named Nordhoff

Major Hirst had to find a German manager for
the factory, a capable person who had not been
too close to the Hitler regime.

Hirst entrusted the management during 1947
to Hermann Münch, a man who ran the factory
more like an accountant than a business executive. Production, which was 7,776 vehicles in
1946, rose to 8,987 units, but more was possible.
The western zone of Germany was unified
administratively that year and a monetary reform
replaced the Reichsmark (which had basically
turned into wastepaper) with the new Deutsche-
mark. Finally, on June 15, 1947, the famous Marshall Plan (named for the American Secretary of
State, George Marshall) was launched to aid the
impoverished countries and provide "the war-
ranties for a stable and prosperous Germany".

On January 1st, 1948, Heinrich Nordhoff replaced Münch, partially at the suggestion of the
Federation of German Automobile Industries.
Nordhoff would guide Volkswagen for another
twenty years, transforming the bomb-scarred
factory in Wolfsburg into the leading European
auto manufacturer and exporter.

When he arrived in Wolfsburg, Nordhoff was
49 years old and, even though he was homeless
and unemployed, he had the reputation of a
competent and tenacious man, a reputation he
had won during his earlier experience at BMW
and Opel in Berlin. He had managed to escape
only a few hours before the Soviets arrested and
deported the entire Opel staff. When Radclyffe
and Hirst contacted him, Nordhoff had found a
modest job in Hamburg as a repairman in an

PRAKTISCHES ZUBEHÖR MACHT IHREN [VW] noch wertvoller

Opel plant. He had never driven a Volkswagen and he had no idea what condition the factory was in. But he accepted unconditionally.

His first action sent Münch packing. "One of the most painful episodes in my life", he would say, and he soon let the British know that he would brook no interference. If he had to manage the factory, fine, he would do so by assuming full responsibility. His speech to the workforce was unyielding and tough: "We are in shit up to our necks. We either get out of it or we drown".

Volkswagen was restructured. First, Nordhoff created three divisions, production, personnel and finance. Soon after, he added a public relations department under Frank Novotny, who was later one of Volkswagen's personnel directors.

Ascher am Schalthebel
Praktisch und für Fahrer und Beifahrer leicht erreichbar.

Ascher in Röhrenform
Leicht am Armaturenbrett des Volkswagens anzubringen.

Anzünder mit Steckdose
Ausreichende Glühdauer auch zum Anzünden von Zigarren

Automatic-Anzünder
Die beheizte Glühspirale schaltet sich automatisch aus.

Rauchergarnitur
mit Uhr, Anzünder, ausziehb. Ascher und Zigarettenhalter.

Handschuhkastendeckel
Verschließbarer Metallklappdeckel mit und ohne Ascher.

Uhr für Handschuhkastendeckel
Von allen Sitzen erkennbare 8-Tage-Uhr m. Leuchtpunkten.

Fernthermometer
mit Steuersäulenhalter und automatischer Signallampe.

Benzinuhr
Wer an sie gewöhnt ist, möchte sie nie mehr missen.

Lenk- und Zündschloß
Diebstahlsicherung, die das Lenkrad automat. blockiert.

The Volkswagen had a rich catalogue of accessories (for that era, of course), as shown here. Numbers two and three are ashtrays; four and five, lighters; six, a dashboard set for smokers (cigarette case, lighter, clock and ashtray); seven, glove box door; eight, clock; nine, thermometer; ten, gas gauge; and eleven, anti-theft device for mounting on the steering wheel.

The second step was signing a contract with Ferdinand Porsche. Volkswagen secured the continued collaboration of the engineer's team and guaranteed him a royalty of ten marks for every Beetle sold, it supplied the Volkswagen-derived parts he needed to begin building sports cars under the Porsche brand. In exchange, Volkswagen obtained an exclusive agreement prohibiting the Porsche studio from designing an economy car, in whole or in part for anyone else.

Nordhoff and his labor force (about 6,000 workers) managed to produce at least 19,244 Beetles during his first year in charge despite the factory's liquidity problems (wages were paid with serious delays) and impossible working

Ihm genügt die „Laternen-Garage":
Original-VW-Lack
macht den Wagen wetterfest!

Above, a Volkswagen ad recommends factory original paints for repairs, because "The lamp post is garage enough". At right, the oval-rear window Beetle produced between 1953 and 1957. Many owners of the split-window model cut away the center mullion to modernize it.

conditions. Workers stood in shin-deep water every time it rained (because the roof had yet to be restored), and they had to set their own fires near the machines and presses when the temperature fell to prevent the hydraulic fluid from congealing.

Nordhoff understood that Porsche's design was remarkably advanced and that every effort should be concentrated on the manufacturing process in order to exploit the great potential of his concepts. The car was not to be altered; instead, they would refine the manufacturing process and the quality of materials. Production had

The oval-window Beetle had a clock in the middle of the dashboard as an accessory. Above right, the anti-glare flipper for night driving is just over the mirror. At left here is the new shape for the oil-bath carburetor filter; engine capacity after 1952 was 1192 cc and 30 horsepower. Right, an eyebrow to concentrate the light beam, and the rear-mounted ski carrier in leather.

tripled by May of 1949, and Beetle number fifty thousand left the Volkswagen assembly line at the end of that month.

In July of that year, the export version was issued. It had hydraulic brakes and improved finishes and was obviously aimed at foreign markets, but could be ordered in Germany for the sum of 5,450 marks. That same month, following a deal with Volkswagen, the automaker Karmann introduced a new cabriolet four-seater, while an open-model Beetle—a two-seater with more elaborate finishes (including a fold-away top) was produced by Hebmüller, another private car maker.

Holland and Belgium were the first countries to import Volkswa-

gens, thanks to an entrepreneurial local merchant named Ben Pon. This Dutch businessman was a force of nature; it was Pon who pushed Nordhoff to manufacture a consumer vehicle and to dare to take the decisive step of selling the Beetle in the United States. Ben Pon and a Beetle weighed anchor from Holland on the motor ship *Westerdam* and landed in New York City on January 17, 1949. Americans, however, were accustomed to ever larger and more powerful cars. The press commonly described the German vehicle as Hitler's car, and the discour-

aged Pon was not only unable to find a distributor willing to import the Beetle, but had to sell his own for $800 to pay his hotel bill. Then it was Nordhoff's turn. He flew to New York with a stack of brochures to publicize the new German car. He introduced himself to Max Hoffman, a

Facing page, top, the consummate symbol of rock'n'roll and the Fifties' urge to be carefree, Elvis Presley. Never before had the appetite for cars mushroomed as it did in that decade, especially in the U.S. Below, the apotheosis of the car, according to *House & Garden*, an American lifestyle magazine, in 1958; the garage opens right into the living room. This page, left, again without a garage, someone has integrated a beloved Beetle into the living room and outfitted it as a reading nook (from *Architectural Digest*, 1998). Above, the *Lightmobile* stands out against a Manhattan backdrop. The work of American artist Eric Staller, its 1600 light bulbs could form 23 distinct configurations. The American flag is by Jasper Johns.

car dealer of German origin who operated in Mississippi. Hoffman added the Beetle to the list of cars he imported from Europe, along with Jaguars and Porsches. The Beetle was offered in four versions: Standard, De Luxe, De Luxe with sunroof or cabriolet (prices ran from $1,280 to $1,997). Hoffmann sold two Beetles in 1949. In 1950, however, demand rose to 330 cars, and hit 980 in 1953. Regardless, Nordhoff was by now convinced not only of the American market's potential, but that he would have to go it alone to establish Volkswagen of America. In the meantime, the domestic market was flourishing. The exacting Volkswagen network, with its exclusive garages and immediate availability of parts, would be Nordhoff's second triumphant weapon, after high quality.

Ernest Hemingway

The famous writer (1899–1961) was among those who came out in favor of the Beetle over the gigantism of American cars (painting by Gil Elvgren, facing page). "At the present moment, it's the best choice", he said. Even today in his beloved Cuba the two automotive phil-

osophies are on view—the Beetle and the Buicks and Chevrolets from the boom years (below and right, photographed on the streets of Havana).

So the time had come. On September 6, 1949, the Volkswagen plant was officially returned to the Germans and became the property of the Federal Republic under the supervision of the State of Lower Saxony. Volkswagenwerk GmBh (Gesellshaft mit beschrankter Haftung, a "limited liability corporation") was born.

Where the Forties were years of revival and consolidation, the following decade was one

of expansion. Especially towards the United States, where the Volkswagen rapidly became a cult car and the highest selling foreign car. To comprehend the Beetle's overseas success, we need a snapshot of American society in the *Roaring Fifties*.

The end of the World War II produced a wave of consumer frenzy in North America fed by a flood of consumer goods from domestic appliances (vacuum cleaners, washing machines, televisions) to clothing and automobiles. Everything had to be fantastic, smell new, look attractive and extravagant. The order of the day was

mobility. And mobility meant being able to work far from home. There was a new trend in the American lifestyle: people had less and less time to get anything done, even to eat.

It's no accident that the McDonald's phenomenon detonated right at the beginning of the decade. American habits were changing—like family composition and the nature of lunch. The midday meal was no longer eaten at home due to a growing distance from the place of work. Mechanization and the standardized manufacture of hamburgers paralleled the assembly line for cars.

But the automobile was the ultimate object of desire, and the new American way of life crystallized around it, famously accompanied by rock and roll. The car was so much a part of the family that garages were designed to "enter" the living room; you could sit on the couch with friends and still admire its muzzle. To consume was to opt

"BILL BERNBACH? HE'S THE MAN WHO FIGURED OUT HOW TO SELL A NAZI CAR TO HUNDREDS OF THOUSANDS OF AMERICAN JEWS."

for freedom and happiness, and the American industry responded by introducing a new model every year. An average car like the 1951 Ford Victoria cost $1,925, had a V8 engine with side valves, 3,923 cc, 100 horsepower, and three gears. It weighed 3,200 pounds and could barely hit ninety mph. The "ride", in short, was the consumer fetish par excellence. It's no coincidence that the pin-up girls drawn by famous American illustrators from Vargas and Gil Elvgren to Art Frahm and Bill Medcalf are posed against hyperbolic hoods.

For all of these reasons the American industry in Detroit—the car capital—was stunned by the blow that Volkswagen delivered against it. The little German car smashed all the rules. It cost only

To make its name in the U.S. market, Volkswagen gave its first ad campaign to DDB for the ridiculous sum of $800,000. Agency creatives saw the Beetle as a relic of Nazism, so they played the irony card. Playing off the American manufacturers who said "Think big", they volleyed "Think small".

Half its beauty is its new, low price!
Makes history by making sense
Exciting new kind of car! Plenty of room for six. Plenty of power without hogging gas. Soundly engineered. Solidly built. And priced with the most popular three!

Think small.

$1,280. Volkswagen did not advertise until 1959 because its executives believed that word-of-mouth was strong enough. In 1955, Volkswagen of America sold thirty thousand vehicles and about seventy-nine thousand in 1957. Eventually, even Nordhoff was persuaded that advertising was the heart of commerce for the average American, and he turned to DDB Needham, whose ad campaign dealt a second blow to the Detroit giants.

The campaign conceived by Bill Bernbach pushed the envelope. One ad was all white and in one corner, at the left, there was a small Beetle. Underneath was a simple sentence, "Think

Left, William "Bill" Bernbach, class of 1911, photographed in 1951. Creative director of the American agency DDB, he invented the slogan "Think small". The Beetle's success was enormous; it quickly became the best-selling foreign car in the U.S. Below, another DDB ad shows Coca Cola and the Beetle, the world's best-known shapes.

small". Rather different from Henry Ford II's dismissive "little shit box," which is what he called the Volkswagen when it showed up in the States. That little box stole market share from the Detroit

2 shapes known the world over.

Nobody really notices Coke bottles or Volkswagens any more.
They're so well known, they blend in with the scenery. It doesn't matter what the scenery is, either. You can walk in and buy a VW in any one of 136 countries. And that takes in lots of scenery.

Deserts. Mountains. Hot places. Cold places. Volkswagens thrive.
Hot and cold don't matter; the VW engine is air-cooled. It doesn't use water, so it can't freeze up or boil over. And having the engine in the back makes all the difference when it comes to mud and sand and snow.

The weight is over the power wheels and so the traction is terrific.
VWs also get along so well wherever they are because our service is as good in Tasmania as it is in Toledo. (The only reason you can't buy a Volkswagen at the North Pole is that we won't sell you one. There's no VW

service around the corner.)
We hear that it's possible to buy yourself a Coke at the North Pole, though.
Which makes us suspect there's only one thing that can get through ahead of a Volkswagen.
A Coke truck.

Below and facing page, two images testify to Germany's recovery in the Fifties, which was symbolized by the Beetle: the Berlin Film Festival in 1954 and the Volkswagen display at the Berlin International Auto Show in 1950. Right, Paul Newman in a testimonial for the Beetle. The famous American actor bought his first Beetle in 1954. Later, Volkswagen showed its gratitude with the convertible in the photograph; to satisfy Newman's passion for speed, the engine was the Porsche 356.

houses in a way they could not fight. And the reason was that, by now, at the end of the Fifties, the American way of life based on planned obsolescence and conspicuous consumption, on mass production and appearances at any cost, was edging toward a crisis.

For a decade consumers had devoured hamburgers and little prefabricated houses and had spent escalating sums to trade in their cars every year. But now the wind was changing, at least for the more upscale public that Volkswagen was aiming for, with a few incursions into the

celebrity world. Paul Newman, for example, came to own four Beetles in Beverly Hills. Volkswagen thought that was enough to ask him for an owner testimonial in 1968.

The Volkswagen was the favorite car of university professors, space engineers, and architects during this period. They were a breed of people who found it utterly uninteresting to pay more for a car. To the contrary, they were quite happy to pay less. The Beetle was also the perfect second car. Detroit denigrated Volk-

in this context that it would be adopted by the hippies, reinforcing the idea of the Beetle as the anti-car.

For Nordhoff the rest of the Fifties beat every forecast. At the end of 1959, production at Wolfsburg reached 553,625 Beetles, and the new Brazilian factory at São Paulo produced another 8,445 units. U.S. sales were a record 84,677 units, but estimates for 1960 exceeded 100,000 vehicles. And in Germany the Beetle filled the cities and towns of the Federal Repub-

Year 1955. Facing page: on Berlin's Kurfürstendamm in front of the ruined Wilhelmkirche, Beetles stood out among cars whose more antiquated design included detached headlights and big vertical radiators. Above left, a long line of Beetles at the border between the two Germanies and, at right, a Beetle whose gas tank was moved to create space in the baggage compartment. About twenty East Germans got through Checkpoint Charlie in this hideout, escaping discovery by the guards.

lic (separated from the GDR after May 8, 1949). Long columns of the little cars crossed the border every day, but only in one direction—from west to east. West Germans were going to see their eastern relatives. In 1961, 818,000 cars were made. That was also the year that the Berlin Wall was built and the Beetle beat another, more meaningful, record. Thanks to one specially customized Beetle, 20 East Berliners crossed into the West without being discovered by the GDR's Vopos (Volkspolizei). Who was going to stop the ugly insect?

swagen buyers as "gray flannel nonconformists", alluding to their penchant for jackets made of tweed rather than a more corporate fabric. In any case, from this moment on in America, the Beetle incarnated the notion of an alternative car with outsider appeal. And it was

As it Was Born, So it is Born

Volkswagenwerk was among the first automotive plants to rationalize production. At the end of the Fifties its buildings stretched 0.9 miles from the fourteen story executive building to the hydroelectric plant. All together, the Volkswagen factory occupied 27,552,000 square feet and devoured thirty-three thousand tons of coal every month. The presses stamped fifteen hundred tons of sheet steel a day, and 1870 tons of magnesium were used to cast the cylinder blocks. At the beginning of the Sixties the presses made five thousand roofs, ten thousand side panels and twenty thousand fenders every day. Everything moved along automatically, pressing, shaping, riveting, and welding the internal and external surfaces. Their assembly took place along conveyor belts that spanned more than sixty miles throughout the plant which eliminated the problem of warehousing individual parts. From engines to tires to car seats, everything was in continuous motion.

After 1957, engine production was moved entirely to Hanover where every line assembled one thousand engines in two sixteen-hour shifts, or one motor every fourteen seconds; Wolfsburg needed forty-three hundred engines a day in 1962. They shipped out of Hanover on a special train 120 cars long.

Above, the assembly line at Wolfsburg in the Fifties and, opposite Beetle fenders; twenty thousand were needed every day. Below, the New Beetle assembly line in Puebla, Mexico.

Beetle shells arrived on overhead conveyor belts for fastening to height of production, one vehicle left Wolfsburg every sixteen seconds assembly according to their destination countries.

The New Beetle being manufactured at Puebla, in Mexico, one of Volkswagen's historical facilities. Among other things, the plant continues to make the old Beetle, which is always in high demand in the domestic market. Production at Puebla is about ninety thousand New Beetles a year.

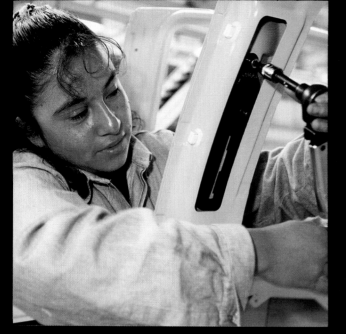

Above, even in a factory as automated as the one in Puebla, half of the final assembly tasks must be done by skilled workers. Below, in the Forties even the rear window was welded by hand.

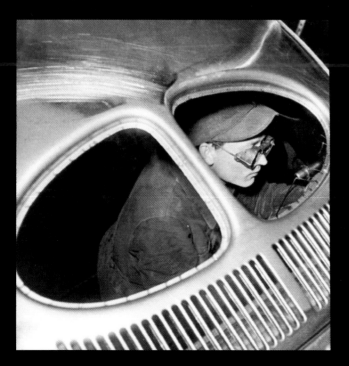

A few official statistics from the Sixties will give an idea of how production was rationalized at Volkswagen. Right after the war, forming the roof took thirty-two minutes and required the deployment of 156 skilled workers and fourteen laborers. Once each task had been mechanized, the same work was finished in 8.4 minutes by forty specialists and fifteen laborers. When welded by hand, it took 52 skilled workers 10.7 minutes to make the hood; the same work was later done by one automatic welder and just twelve skilled workers providing oversight. Even the edges of the bumpers had been burnished by hand; it took 22.5 minutes, and 108 workers were needed for daily production. In 1962, they were machine-finished in 3.6 minutes and eighteen workers produced the same number of parts per day. But rationalization did not stop at the factory. Speedy shipment of the five thousand cars produced every day was guaranteed. Once assembled and inspected, the Beetles were placed in a compartment where a thin layer of wax was sprayed on one vehicle every sixteen seconds. A driver drove it to a parking lot and from there, the cars were loaded by groups onto eighteen trains a day, 420 freight cars long.

And now? Production at Wolfsburg continues to grow but automation is growing even faster. Robots handle 88% of the body work, 70% of the painting, and 50% of the final assembly. The final finishes—the most delicate ones—are left to the workers.

Transgression & Folly

3

POP ART NIBBLED AT IT. THE MOVIES CHEWED IT UP. AND THEY SPAT

IT OUT TRANSFORMED. THE BEETLE WAS NO LONGER JUST A CAR.

IT HAD BECOME A VEHICLE, A MEANS TO REACH EMANCIPATORY,

COUNTER CULTURAL, AND LIBERTARIAN ENDS. ITS DESTINY AS A CAR

FOR EVERYONE AND A FUN CAR HAD FINALLY BEEN REALIZED.

Birth of a Pop Car

It is no coincidence that the Beetle, at the apex of its extraordinary commercial success in the Sixties, was featured in art—especially, Pop Art—even before the movies. The relationship between painting and cars dates back to the infancy of motor cars when the Futurists used automobiles and planes as symbols of a new era, the century of speed. For disciples of Marinetti, from Boccioni to Balla, the automobile, like the airplane, was an aristocratic object. It was difficult to handle, something for the elite. In Pop Art, the relationship was reversed. The

Andy Warhol He demonstrated that every object in daily life has a right to its place in the art world. The only problem is an embarrassment of riches, starting with canned tomatoes and ending with automobiles (at right, the Mercedes 300SL Coupe, 1986). It is no accident that Volkswagen dedicated an important retrospective to Warhol (1930–1987) during the launch of the New Beetle—1998–99.

automobile was simply an article in widespread use. It was a fragment of the everyday world and, as such, it was worthy of celebration. After Marcel Duchamp's transgressions, everything from urinals to cosmetics became artistic. And for the Czechoslovakian Andrew Warhola, known as Andy Warhol, the iconoclastic ex-ad man who celebrated the art of mass-production, the car was perceived and reproduced just like Campbell's tomato soup—as an everyday uniform object. In Warhol's paintings, the Mercedes is repeated in a series and pigmented like an ad and sits next to Marilyn, detergent boxes, women's shoes, flowers, human skulls, Chairman Mao, commissioned portraits of Jacqueline Kennedy, and car crashes with dead people flopping out of shattered windows.

This is America, said Warhol. And he was not the only one. While Warhol portrayed America by painting its objects of mass consumption,

Facing page, Venice Biennial, 1964; one of the most prominent Pop artists, Tom Wesselmann, immortalized with his wife Claire by one of the greatest contemporary photographers, Mario De Biasi. Wesselmann poses in front of one of his "works with everyday objects"—in this case, a Beetle. Right, photographed near San Francisco, the traveling Beetle-Sculpture that was entered in the Artcarfestival of 1996. Note the phrase "Oh My Gawd" on the license plate, a slang way to swear without appearing blasphemous.

Left, evolution of the Beetle in Pop Art continued in Don Eddy's photo-realism (*Untitled*, 1971). Below, art never stops playing with the Volkswagen. These New Beetles were painted during a worldwide contest on the Internet, "New Beetle Gallery". The fourth from left is adorned with the face of Leonardo da Vinci's *Mona Lisa*.

Roy Lichtenstein did the same but using cartoons, the heroes of mass culture. Their contemporary Tom Wesselmann did similar work with everyday objects and mechanical devices. Wesselmann used a little of everything: advertising emblems and neon lights, paints and audio sources, models and reliefs. It was the reproduction of the world as it is, the first step toward photorealism. His paintings reproduced life. He painted bathrooms with radiators, towels and functioning transistor radios stuck to the canvas. And cars in the countryside. Everyday cars. Familiar.

Wesselmann drove the Beetle right into the gallery of western myths. There it is, the Beetle (1964), in an imperturbable physicality surrounded by colors that convey serenity—the sky the color blue of children's drawings, the tree in full leaf, the horizon calm.

The Beetle is an even stronger presence in the work of Don Eddy. Here the point of view is almost that of a child so the car looks about three feet tall. It is as if the Beetle realized who was watching and slowly turned (the rear wheel in fact seems to swerve) and, moving itself, revealed another one right behind it. Again in this example the little Volkswagen comes across

as symbolic of the series but in a hyperrealist dimension quite distant from Tom Wesselmann's familiar one. The car's body shines; the accent falls on its steel and movement. In other words, what is true of art and its objects is true of the sacred and the profane. Any assortment of objects can lend themselves to benediction. It is a question of choices. The same is true for the Beetle, which has another advantage over a can of tomatoes: it moves, it is animated. It can live a life of its own and, thanks to Disney, it finally did.

Indeed, it took that American studio, a specialist in cartoons and family entertainment, to produce a full-length feature in 1969 starring an automobile for the first time in Hollywood and film history. The movies had already employed several objects as "lead actors," of course. Think back to the female android in Fritz Lang's *Metropolis* or Ernst Lubitsch's *Bringing up Baby*. But it had never happened to a vehicle, and certainly not one so popular as the Beetle. It immediately became a star. The film was called *The Love Bug* and was directed by Robert Stevenson.

Despite all this, it still took Woody Allen to land the Beetle in movie history forever. The sophisticated American director had always been enam-

Left, *Carscape* by Erro, 1969. In this work, modern society seems to have no horizon beyond thousands of automobiles. Many Beetles are seen here and there amid the wreckage; the most obvious is the red one at the bottom right.

ored with Europe and its achievements, and he considered the little German car synonymous with an ideological choice. It is an alternative automobile; it is understated and minimalist, just like he is. Its strongest appear-

"THEY REALLY BUILT THESE THINGS, DIDN'T THEY?" WOODY ALLEN, SLEEPER, 1973

and also at a standstill since time immemorial. And which car could it be? The Beetle, of course—a broken-down Bug which naturally starts sputtering happily at the first turn of the key, causing Woody to blurt out,

ance in his films is in *Sleeper* (1973). The protagonist, Woody Allen, wakes up in the distant future after hibernating for 200 years. Hunted by the police, he takes refuge in a cave and there, together with his fiancée, Diane Keaton, he finds a vehicle literally covered with dust and garbage

Above, Woody Allen and Diane Keaton in the film *Sleeper* (1973). This is the famous scene where they discover a Beetle buried in dirt that hasn't been started for two hundred years. Facing page, a sequence from *Annie Hall* (1977) in which

Woody Allen is driven around New York by his fiancée Diane Keaton (who drives like a neurotic.) But no cause for fear; no matter how badly treated, the Beetle convertible escapes unharmed.

"You know, those Germans! If they hadn't fought all those wars. . . ."

In *Annie Hall*, four years later, a white convertible is driven rather rashly by Woody's neurotic fiancée. The sequence showing them driving around New York is memorable and is reproduced here at left.

Returning to Disney, the Herbie saga had a superb script in the best tradition of bright American comedy—in the George Cukor vein, to be precise—with dramatic plot twists, improbable situations, and the inevitable happy ending. Jim Douglas, the human lead, is a fairly unsuccessful racecar driver. After too many crashes to count, he runs off the track yet again and of course wrecks. He is depressed and goes for a walk. He brightens when he sees a beautiful girl, Carole, in a car dealership. Thoroughly flummoxed by so much beauty, he doesn't see the glass and hits his head on the showroom door. Carole comes to his aid and makes him comfortable but while he gathers his wits, Jim is distracted by another miracle (in his eyes), a sports car. While they look each other over—and over again—the real protagonist, Herbie the Beetle, comes out of a second door. He has been abandoned by a rich old lady who bought him for her maid. The dealership is in the hands of the classic Disney bad guy, Mr. Thorndyke, played by David Tomlinson, the same actor who played the harsh and incorruptible father in Mary Poppins. The Beetle disgusts Thorndyke; his penchant is for cars with a pedigree.

Herbie, the Disney Epic

Thorndyke's arrogance brings out Jim's best side. Jim speaks indignantly to Thorndyke who unceremoniously shows him the door. That night, a grateful Herbie abandons the car dealer and parks in front of the house of the unsuspecting driver who, though reluctant, is forced to buy the car to avoid being charged with theft. Jim is forced to take Herbie to the track, but he proves to be a lot faster than anyone had imagined. The film ends with one last showdown between Herbie and the evil Thorndyke who competes in a "real" racecar. The scoundrel, however, had not reckoned with the hidden qualities of Herbie who, when he thinks it's time, takes off at dramatic speeds and passes every car that tries to stop him. The final victory will obviously be Herbie's, and the driver and the girl (disgusted by the tactics of her

© Disney

Facing page, 1969, Herbie, the Beetle according to Walt Disney with the two lead actors, Michele Lee and Dean Jones. *The Love Bug*, directed by Robert Stevenson, achieved worldwide success and launched a series dedicated to the adventures of the famous Volkswa-gen: *Herbie Rides Again* (at left, Goofy with one of the two Beetles used for the film), *Herbie Goes to Monte Carlo*, and *Herbie Lands in Mexico*. Below, a Beetle entered in the real Monte Carlo Rally in 1964.

boss, who doesn't hesitate to get Herbie drunk on Irish coffee in order to win a race) get married.

Just desserts: Thorndyke, who imprudently bet on his own victory with an enterprising Chinese businessman (Herbie's sponsor), loses everything, his money and the dealership, and is reduced to being a mechanic.

The most interesting aspect of this first film that launched the rich Herbie series is that its situations and dialogue reflected many of the contemporary trends in American society: a low-profile demeanor, anti-consumerism, and reassessment of the overall values of Americanism. An example is the conflict between different cultures when the Chinese sponsor bursts in with his benevolent cunning. Another is the move toward the triumph not only of good over evil, but above all of good sense.

Even the dialogue was extremely innovative for Hollywood. The Sixties counterculture movement found its way to the studios, too, even though diluted in comparison to what was really happening on college campuses. For example, the driver has a short fat friend, Tennessee, who has Buddhist inclinations (he has been in Tibet) and is a "professional" sculptor. He creates bizarre compositions by welding together parts of demolished cars. His philosophy is a close relative of Zen: "things" have a soul, too (he is the one who realizes that Herbie is different from other automobiles). He is definitely opposed to the idea of selling Herbie off and replacing him with another car. Tennessee is a representative of a life philosophy that was both uncomplicated and widely shared in the Sixties: "If something works and you like it, why get rid of it? Things get attached to their owners, too. . . ."

One of the reasons for the movie's success, beyond its capable and well-paced direction and despite the sentimental wrapping typical of Disney productions, is its critique of the consumerism in American society.

The *Roaring Fifties*, had left the roads full of vehicles and the souls empty. Once the race for well-being was over, America began to reflect on itself, on its image as a shocking wastrel and world policeman, a society that squandered resources at home and engaged in futile wars to preserve that now-contested supremacy of over-production and hyper-consumption.

The Beetle was even an instrument of self-examination. It allowed the driver to not be obliged to join every contorted political protest and the extravagant libertarian-Marcusian de- mands emanating from Berkeley and vicinity. Quite clearly, the desperation of *Easy Rider* is not on view in *Herbie*; hippies are treated with ironic benevolence and, in line with the Disney philosophy, everything ends with the good guys winning and the equitable (but never excessive) punishment of the bad guys. The Walt Disney Company never fully revealed the tricks it conjured to convert the Beetle into a sports car. Some details are known, however. Partially because a lot of Californian Herbies, as we will see, were subjected to modifications to

Above and left, two images taken from the film, *Herbie Rides Again*. This Volkswagen's mechanical equipment had been highly customized. Though Disney never revealed all of its modifications, we know that the original engine was replaced with a Porsche (as were the brakes). From the Fifties on, and in the United States more than Europe, the Beetle engine was subjected to reconstructive surgery. Below, a typical customization of the "flat-four" or four-cylinder boxer: the capacity goes from 1200 to 2000 cc with two Weber 48 carburetors; horsepower exceeds 120.

boost engine capacity. In fact, Disney technicians replaced the placid four-cylinder engine with the far more powerful 100-horsepower Porsche 356 boxer. 130 mph was available at the touch of the accelerator. The brakes were also Porsches, while the shock absorbers were competition Konis, and the tires had enlarged treads. Thus transformed, Herbie could rear his muzzle in startups from a standstill and lay rubber like a dragster.

Herbie's success was colossal. Volkswagen dealers rushed to stock up on model cars and number-53 stickers to satisfy the demand of thousands who wanted to change their Beetles into so many lighthearted and crazy Herbies.

The Disney series continued with various twists on the original that became less and less persuasive. Among them were *Herbie Rides Again*, *Herbie Goes to Monte Carlo*, and *Herbie Lands in Mexico*. Elsewhere in the film world, Beetle appearances are abundant, starting with

The most famous competition Beetle in the world: the DynoSoar, created for production car races— so beloved in the United States— by Joe Vittone and Dean Lowry, founders of the Santa Ana, California EMPI, a group that specializes in converting Volkswagen cars and engines. The one pictured here is a replica of the original and was produced under Lowry's supervision. The DynoSoar was destroyed in a 1970 attempt to beat the 400-meter acceleration record.

Ingmar Bergman's *Wild Strawberries* (1957) and Stanley Kubrick's *Clockwork Orange* (1971) and up through *The Truman Show* (1998) where a red Beetle helps reveal the deception to which poor Jim Carrey has fallen victim.

Made in the USA: California's Super Beetle

Herbie's success in movie theaters all over the world was not accidental but rather a clear consequence of the Beetle's enormous distribution and popularity. Nothing was easier than seeing oneself in that likable car that was capable of little everyday miracles. Who had not owned or at least driven one? In the U.S., moreover, and especially in California, the modified Beetle fad was already a fairly widespread phenomenon by the mid-Fifties. And it is a tradition that has never ended. Even now enhanced engines and special kits are for sale, and races are held on circular

ment the Beetle's performance, but distribution was sparse. The European motorist, who was more attentive to gas consumption and engine durability, prized safety and longevity while in the States there was a mania for "muscle cars" with 400 horses under the hood.

tracks and dragways (especially in America) between two cars that challenge each other side by side like racing chariots in Roman antiquity.

In Europe, too, and especially in Germany and Great Britain, some manufacturers like Okrasa and Shorrocks, produced converter kits to aug-

And if the eight-cylinder Chevrolet needed enhancing, how could the four-cylinder Volkswagen escape a shot of power? What's more, the Beetle engine was very similar in concept to those of the early Porsches (many of whose parts originally came from Wolfsburg),

A famous Beetle customized in California by Vittone and Lowry, the InchPincher. Like the DynoSoar, this is also a replica of the original, whose trail was lost after an accident. Its engine, pictured above, displaces 1968 cc, and the car's weight is reduced to just 607 kilos.

SORRY 'BOUT THAT

Inch Pincher

EMPI

so mounting a double-barreled carburetor was enough to get the feeling of driving a sports car. The expression "California look," later abbreviated to the more common "Cal-look," was coined by an American journalist who wrote for the magazine *Hot VWs* to define a new fashion that was spreading rapidly around Orange County, a suburb of Los Angeles.

The American passion for customizing the Bug clearly did not end with the Seventies. On this page, a model prepared for the Pro-Stock drag races. Created by Jim Larsen and driven by Greg Brinton, it took the 400-meter record in 1997 at Sacramento, CA in 9.65 seconds.

The distinctive elements of the Cal-look, yesterday and today, are paint jobs that are brilliant in both color and workmanship, the enhanced engine and trim, the squashed-down front-end and oversized tires and wheel rims. This mania was born almost by chance, as a wave of imitation swept through a cluster of American states in the late-Fifties.

Sparking the fire was Joe Vittone, an Italian-American who in 1954 owned a Volkswagen dealership in Riverside, California called European Motor Products Inc.,

Bug-O-Rama In Sacramento at the end of every summer, there is a huge rally dedicated to the Bug and its derivatives, especially the VW bus, which is highly prized on the West Coast. There are drag races between super-customized VWs that arrive from all over the country and many auxiliary events, as well. Not to be missed is the election of Miss Bug; in typical California style, the participants' attributes are manifest.

 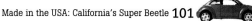

June

soon better known as EMPI. It all got started because Volkswagen did not offer a spare part—the valve seats. Once they wore out, the whole cylinder head had to be replaced. Vittone started to produce valve seats and the instruction manuals for replacing them, and before long they were selling like hot cakes. Then, when the passion for converting engines began to spread among young people after the first Chevrolet V8 was modified in 1956, Vittone imported the Okrasa and Denzel conversion kits (Denzel was an Austrian factory making modified carburetors and blocks that were more expensive and of a higher quality than the Okrasa).

After a modest success, Vittone got down to business. He patented an anti-roll bar for the front end and a stabilizer bar for the rear end, both of which corrected the Beetle's initial ten-

Above and facing page, a Beetle and a VW 1600 TL at the starting line of the Sacramento Pro-Stock drag races. Left, calendars and posters are distributed in California that picture souped-up Beetles and their presumed owners, all of them—inevitably—in bikinis.

dency to tuck under on curves. After 1959, EMPI changed its name, becoming Engineered Motor Products Incorporated. The catalogue included enlarged pistons and cylinders, special exhausts, carburetors, and compressors. The company also built a racing Bug, the InchPincher, with its famous *"Sorry 'bout that!"* slogan. It was designed by Dean Lowry who with his brother Ken would later establish another company that specialized in conversions, DDS. One of the most beautiful competition Volkswagens—the DynoSoar—is credited to them; its logo came from the appealing Hanna Barbera cartoon dinosaur.

It is almost impossible to convey in detail what the Cal-look's hot years represented, even at the technical level. After EMPI and DDS, other companies joined the fray, including Scat or FLAT 4

Performance and the most venerated Beetleist, Gene Berg, now dead, to whom a Memorial Day rally reuniting Volkswagen fans from all over America is now dedicated.

Not one detail of the boxer engine was ignored by these customizers: more powerful camshafts, reinforced and balanced crankshafts, five-speed

July

Left and below, the Dune Buggy is the best-known variation of the Beetle. Its characteristics are an open fiberglass body, roll bar, big wheels, and a souped-up engine. Born to run on long American beaches, they have also had some distribution in Europe. Facing page, the twenty-three-window minibus with three rows of seats was born in 1950 on the mechanical infrastructure of the Beetle.

gearboxes, elongated dimensions, bigger valves, pistons and cylinders as big as 2300 cc, clutches, brakes. . . . In other words, even now anyone who wants to can convert the unassuming Beetle into a little beast with 120 to 180 horsepower that readily scoots past 120 mph.

Parallel to the distribution of special parts for the Beetle, car meets, jamborees and fan clubs were organized all over the United States. The most famous of them was started in California and was first called "Volkswagen Limited" and then "Der Kleiner Panzers", a garble of German and English meaning that the Beetles are little Panzers or bantam armored tanks. The fan clubs grew from one generation to the next and many now have sites on the Internet. But let's go back to the Sixties. Right after 1960, production at Wolfsburg took off, and Nordhoff saw a Volkswagen leave the production line every sixteen to twenty seconds. His motto was that the Volkswagen client always bought more substance than looks.

In 1961, production exceeded a million cars a year, or about 4,200 a day, with a workforce that numbered more than 65,000. 1961 was also the year of important technical modifications. The engine was uprated from 30 to 34 horsepower; the gas tank was redesigned to enlarge the baggage compartment; an automatic starter was installed, and all four gears were synchronized. In 1962 the steering box was improved, the fuel gauge and seat belts were added, and the front hood was counterbalanced with two robust springs that held it open automatically.

In 1964 the canvas sunroof disappeared (replaced by the crank-operated sliding steel roof), the side windows were enlarged, and the nose-shaped license light was abandoned. Finally, in 1965 a more powerful Beetle showed up, the 1,300 cc. Average drivers the world over wanted to drive more impressive cars, but the Volkswagen had a design limitation. The cooling fan revolved twice as fast as the crankshaft, guaranteeing optimal cooling up to 4,000 rpm. And the 1,200 cc engine got up to 3,600 rpm. Alternatives for increasing its power without jeopardizing its life expectancy were minimal. Volkswagen technicians (four hundred of them worked on the car's evolution) could not exceed the 4,000-rpm threshold without drastically altering the fan

claimed to sell more cars than the factory could produce), Volkswagen's chief executive surmised that sooner or later the market would demand something different. The Beetle was twenty years old and could not be improved any further except in its details. And this would never be enough.

In Nordhoff's view, the Volkswagen of the

and pulley, so they increased engine capacity. In 1965, the 1,300 cc version came out with forty horses at 4,000 RPM, and the 1,500 with forty-four horses the following year. The number of revolutions did not change, and front·disk brakes were added while the rear track grew by two inches, from fifty-two to fifty-four inches.

But Nordhoff had to focus on more important things. Even though he liked to say that when things got bad, the last car sold would be a Volkswagen, he had been exploring an alternative to the Beetle for quite some time. Because in reality, and despite the sales records (one ad

future would have to be solid, operate economically, and sell at a good price. Five prototypes of a new car were fabricated in the early Fifties. The simplest one lengthened the Beetle by two inches to capture space for the trunk and passenger compartment, but it was so ungainly that Nordhoff nixed it immediately. The most sophisticated one resembled an Opel sedan even though it preserved the rear engine. Nordhoff was even more hesitant about this model and, without making a decision, he left for a trip that mixed business and leisure in South Africa. After killing a few lions on a safari, he telegraphed his

technicians from there to stop everything they were doing on the new model.

Nordhoff reasoned that producing a bigger car would only lead to worse fuel consumption and higher labor costs, in part because the Beetle engine would no longer be adequate. The new car would have to have a different motor, pushing up design costs and the purchase price.

He also dismissed the idea of designing a smaller, 700 cc car. "Rather than build a subcompact," he said, "we should offer the buyer a Volkswagen that has been used for a year and can be acquired at a price 15 percent lower than a new one. No one can manufacture a 700 cc car at that price that equals the performance of a year-old Beetle."

In the end, a simple product extension to the Transporter and Karmann-Ghia coupe was not enough to brave the second half of the Sixties and the following decade. Even if the single-model Volkswagen embodied many consumer

The commercial vehicle known as the Type 2 was conceived in 1948 by Ben Pon, a Dutch Volkswagen importer, and manufactured two years later. The driver sits over the front axle, the merchandise (or passengers) in the center, and the engine is positioned over rear axle.

The version shown on these pages is the luxury minibus, the model with eight skylight windows and a canvas roof that opens completely. Note, in the little photo on the right, the "Union 76" ball that was given away by distributors of the American gasoline.

advantages (a high used value, easy-to-find spare parts, lower maintenance and repair costs), the mechanism of fashion (that is, the pleasure of changing cars independent of practical returns) was taking hold among drivers. Having survived the critical postwar years, drivers all over the world were starting to find their way to glossier cars that were fun to drive.

However slowly, the values of solidity and economy were going out of fashion. Moreover, Volkswagen's quality standards were much higher than other European manufacturers, and this slowed the development of new models. Suffice to say that every new component had to withstand 62,000 miles of road tests so a certain number of cars were in motion day and night at Volkswagen. They only stopped to get an oil change and undergo the prescribed technical inspections. These endurance tests consumed a lot of time because even if every driver could cover 620 miles a day, it took at least three months to reach the 62,000-mile goal. When the tests were over, the new part might have provided the anticipated results and Volkswagen could put it into production. But if the outcome was negative, everything started over from scratch—calculations, design, fabrication of an experimental model and new tests. These meth-

The world from inside a minibus with its sunroof open. The smaller images at left and right compare it with the Beetle and show that German technicians kept the outside dimensions of the minibus extremely compact. It only extends a little beyond the front and side profiles of the Volkswagen sedan.

Facing page, an ad launching the 1500 cc, 44 horsepower model of 1966. Its top speed (and the cruising speed, as always) is 75 mph. It was the first Beetle to use front disk brakes.

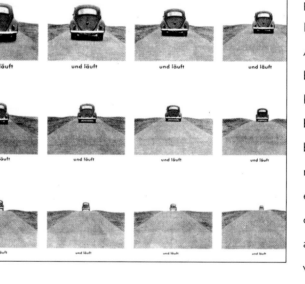

Warum werden so viele Volkswagen gekauft?
(Bis heute 6 Millionen: 3 Millionen in Deutschland. 1 Million in Amerika. 2 Millionen in der übrigen Welt.)
Dafür gibt es viele Gründe. Das ist der wichtigste:

Der VW läuft — und läuft — und läuft — und läuft — und läuft — und läuft — und läuft — und läuft — und läuft — und läuft — und läuft — und läuft — und läuft — und läuft — und läuft — und läuft

Left, the most famous Volkswagen ad for the Beetle: "The VW goes" "and goes" "and goes" "and goes" "and goes" . . .

ods sustained the constant evolution of the Beetle, which became more reliable and robust but changed very little on the outside. But the consumer wanted more external innovation. The car was becoming a rapidly replaced asset.

Nordhoff commissioned Porsche to study a new car in collaboration with the Ghia coach factory. In 1957 the general lines were sketched in and the Type 3—commonly called the VW 1500—was presented to the public at the Frankfurt Auto Show of September 1961. The chassis had the same wheelbase as the Beetle but the body had been redesigned. The new edition models were completely new and available in a family version or coupe. Rated at 1500cc and forty-five horsepower, the engine was very compact, with the fan fitted directly

Revolt of the savers On October 7, 1948, Karl Stolz, center, founded the Association of Former VW Savers, those 337,000 Germans who bought savings stamps during World War II to reserve a Beetle. Stolz's Association asked Volkswagen to recognize its debt and discount a new Beetle according to the amounts deposited. The case was pursued through 1961, when a compromise was reached. VW expropriated the money that had been handed over to the KDF and discounted the price of a car by 150 to 600 marks.

VW 1500 SPORT

**Breitere Spur!
Ausgleichsfeder!
Stärkerer Motor!
Scheibenbremsen!
Startet schneller!
Überholt schneller!
Bremst
schneller!**

AG
56043

AMAG
*Generalvertretung
Schinznach-Bad*

onto the engine to reduce its height to just fifteen inches. This allowed for two baggage compartments, one in front and one over the engine.

Unfortunately, its performance in terms of speed was still modest. Its maximum (and cruising) speed was seventy-five mph, but gas consumption slid down to eighteen or twenty miles per gallon. It was not an economy car but it was also too modest to grapple with more patrician brands like the Lancia, Alfa Romeo, or Peugeot.

Moreover, the Type 3 cost one fifth more than the Beetle and, though it offered more space, it simply looked out of date and it failed to excite either the trade press or drivers.

Einen VW müsste man haben.

Einen VW müsste man haben.

VW 1500 that was supposed to supersede the Beetle continued through 1973 for a total of 2,585,000 units. Volkswagen's first attempt to leave the single-model policy behind had been half a failure.

Manufacture of the Beetle continued at more than one million units a year: Volkswagen had no other road to take. But Nordhoff knew that

In 1966 the Type 3 was offered in the 1600 TL version, which was also called the fastback. Its aesthetics were visibly improved, but its engine was quite a bit thirstier for gasoline. Production of the

Above, the coupe manufactured by the autobody maker Karmann along the lines of the Italian Ghia; the first version dates from 1953, and the one pictured is the 1968 convertible with 1500 cc engine.

Above left, the launch ad for the new VW 1600 TL "fastback" (1966) pictured below: it had a new air-cooled, 54 horsepower rear engine.

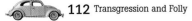

sooner or later even "old faithful" would have to retire, and the factory at Wolfsburg risked finding itself ill prepared for that eventuality.

In the meantime, the German firm was growing internationally. In 1964, Nordhoff established a new branch in Mexico at Puebla and the same year, on October 23, he bought a German factory that was in trouble but had a lot of designs in the drawer. This was Auto Union, previously owned by Daimler-Benz, which united some of the more glorious—if forgotten—trademarks in German automotive history, Audi, Wanderer, Horch, and DKW.

The year of global protest, 1968, was memorable for Volkswagen. In 1966 and 1967, Beetle production had fallen considerably, dropping from 1,085,165 vehicles to 925,786. For the first time, Beetles were left unsold in the United States and therefore offered at sale prices at the end of the year.

A turnaround was essential. Unable to devise a true alternative, Volkswagen technicians wagered on a complete rethinking of the car designed by Ferdinand Porsche.

The new 1968 Beetle had more effective vertical headlights, new and decidedly stronger steel plate bumpers, an external gas tank inlet (no longer under the hood) protected by a small flap, dual-circuit braking, and seats that were finally more ergonomic. Above all, it abandoned the 6-volt electrical system in favor of the 12-volt, which a majority of manufacturers had already adopted. Because the Bosch dynamo furnished power in proportion to the rpm, the 6-volt system allowed the voltage to drop over time. If the headlights were on and the engine at minimum revs, the turn indicators would not work or the horn dimmed.

VW Cabriolet The Beetle was first conceived in three versions: sedan, sunroof, and convertible or "cabriolet". The first "cabrio" was given to Adolf Hitler and is now in the Wolfsburg Museum. After the war, in 1949, Volkswagen commissioned two separate car makers to manufacture two different convertibles. Hebmüller was to produce the two-seater version (Type 14A) and Karmann, the four-seater (with a top that lay outside the body once it was folded back, a Type 15). The Hebmüller version (similar to the one built by the workers in 1945 for the British command) was the first

to appear, but it did not last long. A fire in 1950 devastated the assembly hall and Nordhoff (who found Hebmüller unpleasant) did not renew the contract. The Karmann convertible, instead, was produced until January 10, 1980, at a total of 300,000 units. In the postcard, the pink "cabrio" is the 1303 model (1973, known as the Super Beetle); it can be identified by the larger, more rotund hood (the bumper guards were accessories).

(Type 4) in August of 1968 as a "completely new" car. In fact, the chassis was unibody, the McPherson suspension was state of the art, but the machinery remained the same. The rear engine with its same four cylinders was boosted to 1700 cc and 68 horsepower, giving the car a top speed of ninety mph. It was soon followed by a version called the Variant with even more power (eighty-five horses) and supplied with electronic injection. Its gas consumption, however, was even higher; at top speed it could gulp a little over a gallon for every fifteen miles. And then, like the VW 1500, the new line not only failed to elicit enthusiasm but was actively rejected. In all, just 211,000 of the 411 were sold (production ended in 1974, the year that the Golf, the true heir to the Beetle, was introduced).

Heinrich Nordhoff was not destined to face the difficult era between the end of the Sixties and the early Seventies. After announcing that he would retire on December 31, 1968, he died on April 12 of that year after more than twenty years in charge.

The Beetle's sales revival starting in 1968 could not be wholly explained by the technical improvements that were introduced. The third childhood of the people's car had cultural roots and triggers. If during the Fifties you could be taken for a Harvard intellectual by wearing a flannel cap and driving a Beetle, that same car was now chosen to demonstrate one's complete alienation from consumer society. The movement generically defined as "The Sixties" was born in the United States, exported to France

The Passionate Years

Despite Volkswagen's emphasis on its revolutionary 1968 model, everything on the mechanical side was unchanged. Volkswagen still believed in the air-cooled rear engine that was proof of the car's old age. More important, though, they were still missing improvements like forced-air ventilation (which was only added in 1970); when it rained, you had to travel with the wing-windows open to defog the windshield.

The new Beetle was well received, nonetheless, and production began to grow again in 1968 to more than 1,100,000 units. Efforts to find alternatives to the single model were still destined to fail, however. After the VW 1500, Wolfsburg decided to bet on a larger vehicle again, and they ceremoniously launched the VW 411

In the second half of the Sixties, the Beetle became the symbolic car of the youth protest movement. The vehicle's rounded shape lent itself to personal and defiant or transgressive colors and exhibitions. Above, an image by Eliot Erwitt. Many women adopted the same style as Janis Joplin, the beautiful and damned rock singer (large photo, facing page). But 1968 was also the year of significant technical innovations. The new model at right has vertical headlights, steel-plate bumpers, flat hubcaps, and a 12- rather than 6-volt electrical system.

A force d'être démodé, on finit par être à la mode.

Easy Rider.

Volkswagen rode the youth wave of the Sixties with no hesitation. Left, two images that capture the mood of those years: the first reads, "By constantly being out of fashion, one ends up being all the rage". The second evokes the famous film *Easy Rider* with Peter Fonda, Dennis Hopper and Jack Nicholson. Below, a graphic pun between the symbols for anarchy and the Volkswagen. Facing page, the Kurfürsterdamm, in Berlin on April 30, 1968; the shoes of student leader Rudi Dutschke, who had just been injured in an attack, abandoned in front of a Beetle.

for the famous events of May 1968, and spread from there to other European countries, first at the student level and then among workers. (To recall the era we chose a dramatic image of the attack on "Red Rudy" in Berlin, whose sole witness is rightly a Beetle). The Sixties adopted two cars that were the antithesis of social ostentation and display, the *deux cheveux* Citroen and the Beetle. The diminutive Volkswagen found special favor among women who were gaining personal mobility along with the right to speak for themselves. Beetle headquarters was not blind to this liberal appropriation of its car. Quite the contrary. It hopped on board and staked its advertising on messages that abandoned the classical middle-class family audience to address the counterculture directly. A typical ad of the time showed four kids dressed in Sixties fashion

with exaggerated jeans, jackets and hair around a Beetle. By constantly avoiding fashion, it said, the Beetle has become fashionable. And in the same communicative vein, Beetles are pictured with symbols of anarchy and the hippie world. There was even a denim version with an interior lining in psychedelic colors. But the Beetle era was still heading for sunset. Before ceding its place to the Golf in July of 1974, Volkswagen found yet another way to re-launch the 1302 (1971) and 1303 (1973), known as the Super Beetle or Super Bug.

The Super Beetle was immediately distinguishable from the Beetle by a bulbous nose that was two inches longer and by new McPherson struts replacing the torsion bars. The combination of these two elements allowed for a horizontal spare tire and a considerable increase in

Left and below, two images that open and close the Beetle's golden age. The advertising poster shows Beetles leaving German docks for markets all over the world during the Fifties; the photograph, however shows the last Beetles produced in Mexico for the European market as they are unloaded at the German port of Emden near the Dutch border in 1985.

the front baggage compartment. Its capacity nearly doubled to 2.7 cubic yards.

Unfortunately, the extra weight and the longer dimensions came at the expense of fuel consumption and further penalized the Volkswagen's already less than dazzling performance. To travel at a cruising speed that was more in line

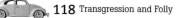

The end of an era

Left, the last Beetle produced at Wolfsburg, July 1, 1974. Production was transferred to Emden and continued until January 19, 1978. Above, the Super Beetle 1303 made in 1973, with its panoramic windows and, beside it, the Jeans model, a limited-edition Beetle (1974). Below, French ad from 1972; two Beetles take their place in line for Noah's Ark.

with newer cars and in different traffic situations, a new 1600 cc, 50 horsepower engine was proposed.

The Super Beetle 1303 differentiated itself from all other Beetles and Super Beetles by a new curved windshield (50 percent larger) which, together with a new dashboard made of shock-absorbent plastic, made the passenger compartment seem larger and airier. The last Beetle left Wolfsburg on July 1, 1974. Production of just two versions—the 1200 and the 1600—was limited to the factory at Emden. The Super Beetle disappeared the following

year. Production continued until January 19, 1978, when Volkswagen shut down the assembly line at Emden as well, and started importing one model from Mexico, the 1200 A. It had a padded dashboard, head rests, and standard thermal rear window. On January 10, 1980 assembly of the Karmann convertible at Osnabrück was also terminated.

Halfway through 1985, a final batch of 3,600 Beetles in gun-metal gray was unloaded in Europe. Called the Jubilaeus Käfer, it celebrated the fifty years since the first prototypes. Then Mexican imports stopped forever.

4

Resurrection

So what, in the end, is the Beetle? The most produced car. The best-loved car. The most reproduced car. The car that outlived itself, capable of rebirth even before it died. And the car that, glorying with a "New" in front of its name, shifts into the new millennium, a happy inheritance from the 20th Century.

 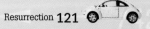

Perpetuating the Myth

The Beetle is not only the world's most produced car—twenty million sales worldwide—
but it is also the most reproduced—on every
possible scale imaginable from the moment
of its conception. Ferdinand Porsche himself
had three 1:25-scale models made to show
Hitler the final lines of the new automobile. In
1949, the workers at Wolfsburg constructed a little green model as a memento of their regard
for Major Ivan Hirst who had put Volkswagen
back on its feet (the miniature Beetle is preserved under glass at the Major's house in Mars-
den, England).

But apart from these unique and noncommer-
cial fabrications (one of Porsche's models was
even auctioned at Christie's) and ever since the
Forties, many toy companies have reproduced
the Beetle. While a detailed history of the

author's love affair with models would fall
beyond the scope of this book, I have nonetheless insisted on giving the reader a short
overview of mini-Beetles by introducing some
of the rarest items on the model market, thanks
to the collaboration of two Italian collectors and
experts, Marco Battazzi and Massimo Tentori.
Remembering that prices escalate in this
market, current prices run from $30 for less
precious models to $350 for the rarest ones
dating to the Forties and Fifties. Maximum
value is always tied to the model's perfect con-

Left, wind-up split-window Beetle in
steel, TippCo mark, 1:45 scale; Germany, 1947. It sold with a seg-
mented metal track for use as a road-
way. Above, *Das Gläseme
Auto* (the see-through
car), a Volkswagen
promotional model
with the oval rear win-
dow, made of plastic. Wiking
mark, 1:40 scale; Germany, 1958.

Above and left, center, a diecast twenty-three-window minibus with plastic parts and a folding canvas roof, 7" (180 mm) long, 1:25 scale, Franklin Mint mark; USA, 1993. Above left, VW promotional Beetle in plastic, 1:40 scale, with original box, and a red Beetle with a plastic body and metal interiors, friction driven, 1:20 scale, Arnold mark; Germany, 1949. Lower left, Wiking promotional model VW from the Fifties. Below, TippCo model, 1:30 scale; Germany, circa 1949.

dition and the (obligatory) presence of the original packaging.

The big wind-up Beetle made in 1947 by Tipp-Co is among the oldest. Spring-action models with a metal shell also had metal wheels but were sold with rubber tires in some cases.

Made in the last years of the Forties, the first plastic models—that still have a metal under-

Left, metal Kübelwagen 1:25 scale, 6 _" (163 mm) long, Gonio mark; Czech Republic, 1990. Below, split-window Beetle, 1:90 scale, 19" (476 mm) long, Wiking mark; Germany 1948. Photomontage below, Ferdinand Porsche admires the New Beetle (Bburago, 1:25, Italy). Facing page, Peruvian Beetle in clay, approx. 1:25 scale (but they exist in every size).

body and interiors—are also highly sought after, like those by Arnold and the later plastic Wikings from the Forties and Fifties. Wiking, in fact, manufactured models at 1:40 scale exclusively for Volkswagen. Later, it made a series of models in the scale of HO model electric trains, first as decoration for the train sets and eventually as a collection in and of itself. Beetle-lovers ought to know that Wiking made every variant of the famous car at 1:90 scale.

"THE MOST COLLECTIBLE TOY BEETLES? THEY'RE THE METAL ONES MADE IN THE FORTIES AND FIFTIES."

The Portuguese brand Vitesse now carries the most versions and variations of the Beetle in its catalog, including the military ones and the New Beetle, which has also been recreated exceptionally well by the Italian company Bburago at 1:25 scale in the three primary colors, blue, red and yellow.

Noteworthy reproductions of the Beetle and its derivatives are also made in former Communist bloc countries (such as those from the former Czechoslovakian factory Gonio) and in Japan, Korea, Hong Kong and, inevitably, even in China.

In the absence of a collector's obsession, however, an irreverent alternative can be found in the work of artisans, especially from Latin

Variations on a theme: Volksplanes, or airplanes with Beetle engines, were common in the United States among devotees of light aircraft and were often hand built at home. The boxer engine with its finned and protuberant cylinders, in fact, lends itself well to this type of work.

America. From Mexico to Peru and as far south as Argentina, the Beetle surfaces in the most comical and diverse materials (like the clay Peruvian shown on the preceding page). In the end, since the Beetle has so thoroughly saturated our history, it is only normal to find it more or less everywhere, a happy and spirited icon.

But let's get back to the history because, even if we are approaching the end, the last word has not been written. And it may never be. Ignoring the New Beetle's high-tech resurrection, we can start from the fact that the assembly lines in Mexico and Brazil have never shut down and that they continue to churn out forty to fifty thousand Beetles for the domestic market (plus one hundred thousand New Beetles).

Left, 1985, a group of Mexican workers pose at the Puebla factory with the last Beetle exported to Germany. Below, 1986, the Jubilee Beetle commemorating the 50th anniversary of the first Volkswagen prototype. Issued in a limited edition, it was a metallic gunmetal gray color. It has a high market value.

Following the rock and roll and rebellion years, the steadfast Mr. Beetle had to face the big tribulation of the Eighties. On May 15, 1981, the twenty-millionth Beetle left the Puebla assembly line in Mexico. A limited edition called the Silver Bug was put together to celebrate the event; it was a metallic silver with more refined interior and a black band at the bottom of the doors. It had the classic 1.2 liter, 34 horsepower engine. Beetle exports from Mexico to Europe continued until 1985, encompassing special editions like the Special Bug in metallic black paint with gold-colored wheel rims at the end of 1982, and the Flower Bug in June of 1983 that was eggplant colored right down to the wheel rims.

The last shipment of 3150 Mexican Beetles was unloaded in Germany on August 12, 1985 for sale at the truly restrained price of 11,130 marks. Despite protests from the fan clubs, Volk-swagen no longer had a commercial interest in selling the Beetle in Europe. Moreover, to comply with new laws limiting pollution from auto emissions, the company would have had to modify the engine inordinately, making the operation completely uneconomical. What's more, Volkswagen's new president, Karl Hahn, who was appointed in 1982 after many years with Volkswagen of America, was convinced that the House of Wolfsburg should make a clean break and essentially forget that it had been the House of the Beetle—always and only—for nearly 40 years.

In any case, a final special edition was put together in 1986 with some of the Beetles that came in from Mexico. It was called the Jubilaeus

Käfer—the Jubilee Beetle—to celebrate the 50 years' existence of the car for the common man.

Its color was gunmetal gray, as were the interior materials; the wheel rims were pressed steel, and the blueish windows were energy efficient. The seats and the steering wheel were taken on loan from the Golf GTI.

Mexican Beetle imports continued but through private commercial brokers. The available model had a 1600cc, 44 horsepower engine with electronic fuel injection and a catalytic converter that could be sanctioned in all the European countries. Only a few dozen units were ever imported, however, because the price had risen enough to

Ferdinand Piëch
Class of 1938, president of Volkswagen since 1993, and nephew of Ferdinand Porsche, is the father of the New Beetle. The Volkswagen Group (1998) has sold at least 4,447,818 vehicles around the world (VW, Bentley, Rolls-Royce, Seat, Audi, and Skoda). Below, a model of Autostadt, the futuristic City of the Car constructed on a cast-off industrial site at Wolfsburg on the occasion of Expo 2000 in Hanover. Autostadt is a city of wonders created in homage to the world of Volkswagen from the Beetle and on into the future. A great plaza welcomes visitors who can choose from movie theaters with 360-degree 3-D screens, an auto museum, a shopping area, showrooms, restaurants, and a "Beetle Mecca".

The first prototype of the New Beetle, fabricated in California in 1994. It was called the Concept One and its final version (modified for safety reasons) clearly evoked the lines and design of the old Beetle, including the two little grills on the front; one was purely cosmetic and the other camouflaged the horn. From the beginning, the New Beetle's dashboard took inspiration from the Beetle's big circular instrument; so did the steering wheel, which was altered to hold an air bag. The Concept One had a transparent roof that was later abandoned.

discourage even the most inveterate fans. On June 23, 1993, Puebla took the Beetle to another record high at 21 million units, but the real surprise was still to come. Six months later, at the 1994 Detroit Auto Show, Volkswagen presented the Concept One. It was a study from California—the native soil of design and innovation—of what a contemporary Beetle could be, right down to the engine in front.

The Concept One was strongly backed by the new president at the

House of Wolfsburg, Ferdinand Piëch, class of 1937, nephew of Ferdinand Porsche, and already head of Audi.

Volkswagen had long since established a center for car design in Simi Valley, California. Soon after the Concept One, it prepared a convertible version for the Geneva Auto Show and another, more definitive, version in glossy black for the Tokyo Auto Show of 1996.

Orders for the New Beetle, the preselected name, were sufficiently encouraging for Plech

Facing page and at right, frontal and rear views of the Concept One in a semifinal version presented at the Tokyo and Geneva Auto Shows, respectively, in 1995 and 1996. Compared to the original, it has been lengthened to better meet U.S. safety regulations. Below, superimposed, the skeleton of the old on the New Beetle. The New Beetle is about the same size; it is shorter in height and length, but has a longer wheelbase (the distance between the wheels) for greater comfort.

to decide to put the car into production right away. The assembly line was set up at Puebla, and sales started in the United States in 1998 and a year later in Europe.

Compared to the first model, its proportions were slightly elongated to give the engine more room and to integrate the bumpers which, according to U.S. market norms, had to withstand light collisions at speeds up to five miles an hour without damage (and the U.S. market was critical to the launch of the New Beetle in the view of Volkswagen officials). Developing the car

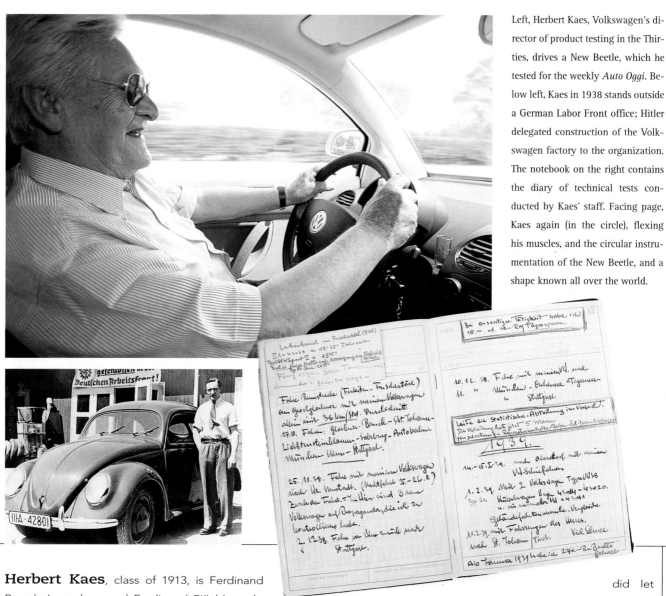

Left, Herbert Kaes, Volkswagen's director of product testing in the Thirties, drives a New Beetle, which he tested for the weekly *Auto Oggi*. Below left, Kaes in 1938 stands outside a German Labor Front office; Hitler delegated construction of the Volkswagen factory to the organization. The notebook on the right contains the diary of technical tests conducted by Kaes' staff. Facing page, Kaes again (in the circle), flexing his muscles, and the circular instrumentation of the New Beetle, and a shape known all over the world.

Herbert Kaes, class of 1913, is Ferdinand Porsche's nephew and Ferdinand Piëch's uncle. He traveled thousands of miles in the grueling Beetle road tests of the Thirties. After the War, he raced the first Porsche competition cars and later tested every successive model up through the late Seventies. The weekly magazine, *Auto Oggi,* asked him to test the New Beetle. Kaes gladly accepted. And he liked it. Here are his impressions. "The engine is front traction, I know. And look how fast it is! Porsche had it in back because that was the only system that would meet the price level imposed by Hitler; it did let us get by without the drive shaft. It was air cooled to guarantee mechanical reliability. You can't imagine the problems we had with water cooling. The line of the New Beetle is the ideal elaboration of the old one. The trunk is smaller, though. That is really funny. The old one held more stuff, even if German workers vacationed at most twelve days a year and right when they got married. . . . The instrumentation is like the one back then, and the driver's position is good, but the pillars cut down visibility. Just like in the old one."

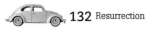

had consumed almost $2 billion. In designing the body, Volkswagen followed the old Beetle's roundish lines as closely as possible, simultaneously working to uphold contemporary aerodynamic standards. The result is that the New Beetle has a CX of 0.38, less than the famous 0.40 achieved by the Beetle in the wind tunnel in 1938, but without wheel covers and with streamlined wheels.

The unitized body in zinc-coated steel has an enormous torsional rigidity and is guaranteed against rust for twelve years. The bumpers and fenders are resin while the rest of the body is

Above, frontal dimensions of the New Beetle, about 8 inches (20 cm) wider than the old Beetle. At right, a three-quarter rear view of the New Beetle; the trunk lock is under the VW logo. Facing page, the New Beetle proposes to bring back the flower vase, a typical Fifties accessory.

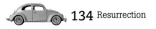

steel. They are painted simultaneously by a system that guarantees the same color tonalities despite the difference of materials. As on the old Beetle, the New Beetle's fenders are bolted on so they are easy to replace in case of collision.

Name and style aside, the differences between the two cars are so striking that fans of the old Beetle have screamed betrayal. The underpinnings and engines (a 2000 cc, 115 horsepower gasoline—with automatic transmission in the U.S.—and a 1900 turbo diesel at 90 horsepower) are the

"I REALLY WANTED THE NEW BEETLE AS AN HOMAGE TO MY GRANDFATHER, FERDINAND PORSCHE" FERDINAND PIËCH, 1998

outset, produced in 100,000- to 120,000 units (at least for the first two years) and destined to be more of a toy car than a people's car, especially in Europe, where people consider a 2000 cc engine the prerogative of higher-class sedans.

The only trait that unites the two Beetles, beyond the superficial resemblance sought and largely achieved, is their internal space. The New Beetle's trunk barely equals the sum of the two baggage units in the old Bug (the nose compartment and the well behind the rear seat) even if the tail-

same as the Golf, obviously fluid cooled, and the traction is front-end. The New Beetle shares all the amenities of other modern cars from air conditioning to air bags and the ABS brake-control system. It is a sumptuous car whose price is ultimately moderate at $18,000 to $19,000. So, while the Beetle was an austere vehicle destined for immense distribution, the New Beetle was clearly a niche car from the

gate and the adjustable seats increase its size. The passengers have about the same elbow room in both cars. Though it only promises to transport four people and not five like the "old faithful," everything is clearly more rational in the New Beetle. And . . . very important . . . one of the old Beetle's worst traits has been eliminated—the howl of the air-cooled boxer engine that made it impossible

to hear music and very hard to make oneself heard over sixty mph.

Travel by Beetle is now far superior in many ways. The biggest old Beetle engine, the 1600, could barely get past eighty-five mph while the New Beetle cruises at 110 and its gas consumption is undeniably better, especially in the diesel version. The gasoline engine allows the New Beetle to go from zero to sixty mph in 10.9 seconds and gets twenty-seven miles per gallon. The diesel version goes from zero to sixty mph

the oldest Beetle Club, the Volkswagen Owner's Club of Great Britain, founded in 1953) to Japan.

Even Volkswagen seems to be aware of the contradiction and has already decided to produce a Light version of the New Beetle with a smaller engine and fewer accessories to keep the price under $15,000.

In the summer of 1999, another news report caused Beetle-lovers' hearts to leap; the New Beetle was photographed in California with a

in thirteen seconds and consumes even less, getting forty-eight miles per gallon on the highway. An old Beetle fitted with a Solex carburetor in place—even though it is hard to maintain the correct calibration—can go thirty to thirty-three miles on a gallon of gas on the highway and twenty-three in the city.

The high purchase price has disappointed thousands of Beetle fans, especially the young ones, who belong to innumerable clubs scattered all over the world from Russia to the U.S., from Italy (Club Amici del Maggiolino, 1976) to Sweden, and from Great Britain (which boasts

rear engine. It was the classic four-cylinder air-cooled model mounted on a VW 411, a 1800 cc with an enlarged fan and 85-90 horsepower. In France a petition asking Volkswagen to produce and import the New Beetle Light was immediately launched via the monthly *VW Magazine*. Hundreds responded, but it was only a joke.

Wherever the New Beetle adventure takes us, the irreducible fact is that the Beetle meets the new millennium as the true car of the last century. The 20th century would not be what it was without the people's car. Will the same be true of the 21st?

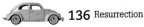

Is this the end?

Sixty Years of Constant Mutation

Despite its seemingly immutable form, no car has ever weathered as many modifications in its lifetime as the Beetle.

Between the first model manufactured in 1938 and the last exported to Europe in 1986, not one detail stayed the same, with the exception of the chassis and the overall dimensions.

The mechanical equipment was constantly perfected from the size of the clutch to the capacity of the oil pump to the ventilation. Some detail was improved almost every year.

From 1955 on, adopting the American industry's practice, innovations were always introduced during the plants' summer closure in August.

Taking advantage of summer vacations, technicians could adjust the assembly line to produce the new car. Thus, the 1956 model year was introduced in August of 1955 and so on. So the 1965 Beetle appeared in 1964. When looking for a particular modification, you always have to remember to look at the chassis number so you don't mistake the year. Here are the principal modifications of the Käfer.

1946 First model, Type 11, 1131 cc, 25 horsepower. Identical to the prewar model that was never really put in production.

7·1·1949 Birth of the Export model, high-gloss paint job, chrome trim, front hood could be opened from inside with a safety lock.

4·28·1950 Type 11A model, operable canvas sunroof optional.

1·6·1951 Side air intakes for ventilation, telescopic rear shock absorbers, enameled Wolfsburg crest on the rear hood, cushioned armrests for the rear seat (only on

the Export model and only at the end of 1951).

10·1·1952 Smaller wheels (5.60-15"), vent windows, bumpers and bumper guards modified, two brake lights combined with position lights and turn-signal indicators.

3·10·1953 Enlarged oval rear window with no central mullion.

12·21·1953 New 1192 cc, 30 horsepower, 3400 RPM, 7.7 mkg engine. Started with a key rather than a button on the dashboard.

The breaking-in period for the engine is eliminated.

8·1·1955 Double exhaust pipe, sunroof in plastic fabric, new rear lights and turn signals mounted higher on the back fenders. U.S. regulation reinforced bumpers introduced.

8·1·1957 Rear window and windshield enlarged, new shape for the rear hatch lid, nose-shaped hood over the rear license light.

8·1·1958 External rear view mirror standard.

8·1·1959 Stationary door handles with pushbutton operation. Anti-roll bar on the front axle.

8·1·1960 Window-cleaner mechanism, asymmetrical low-beam lights, semaphore turn signals replaced by flashing bulbs, 1192 cc, 34 horsepower, 3600 RPM, 8.4 mkg engine, automatic starter. Tank enlarged from 22 to 36 gallons.

8·1·1961 Rear lights in two sec-

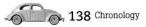

tions. Fuel gauge, counterbalanced front hood.

8·1·1962 Wolfsburg crest eliminated from the hood.

8·1·1963 Crank-operated sliding steel sunroof, larger and rectangular cowling over the license light.

8·1·1964 Glass surface area enlarged; windshield wipers rest on the left, engine hood opened by pushbutton.

8·1·1965 Perforated wheel rims,

8·1·1967 12-volt electrical system, vertical front headlights, new ventilation system, three-point anchoring of the seatbelts, rear belts, plastic knobs, steel-plate (stronger) bumpers, external fuel inlet on right side.

8·1·1970 New model, nicknamed the Super Beetle (imprint 1302) with enlarged baggage compartment and horizontal rather than vertical spare tire. McPherson-

8·1·1973 The 1303 has a negative ground. Standard Beetle with bumpers painted black.

8·1·1974 Rear turn indicators no longer on the fenders but integrated into the bumpers.

8·1·1975 Beetle L with chrome bumpers and hub caps, rims painted silver, backup lights, forced-air ventilation, padded dashboard.

8·1·1978 End of sedan model

flat rather than rounded hubcaps, new 1300 cc engine, letter F, 40 horsepower (the 34 horsepower, 1192 cc engine becomes letter D; the 30 horsepower A is for the economical Standard version).

8·1·1966 New 1500 cc engine, letter H and 44 horsepower, rear track enlarged, rear hood modified, license light changed, thinner chrome molding, new door locks. Disk brakes on the front wheels standard for the 1500, optional for the 1300.

style front suspension.
New engines: 50 horsepower 1600 cc (letter AD), and 44 horsepower 1300 cc (letter AB). Dynamic circulation with forced rear flow on the Beetle, too.

8·1·1971 Better ventilation, supplementary air intakes on the rear hood.

8·1·1972 New Super Beetle (imprint 1303) with panoramic windshield and new curved dashboard. Rear window surfaces enlarged.

production in Germany; Mexican-made Beetle begins export to Europe.

8·1·1985 Beetle imports from Mexico terminated.

January·1994 Concept One presented at the Chicago Auto Show and another version at the Tokyo Salon of 1995; definitive version of the New Beetle appears at the Geneva Auto Show in 1996.

Spring·1998 The New Beetle is merchandised in the U.S. and after 1999 in Europe.

Index of Names

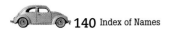

Bibliography

The following is a minimal list or reasoned bibliography of basic texts for anyone who wishes to get further acquainted with and maybe even study the historic and more strictly automotive aspects of the Volkswagen.

For the Middle European social climate and history of the Nazi dictatorship:

Bolaffi Giulio, *Il Sogno Tedesco*, Donzelli Editore, 1993.

Corni Gustavo, *Storia della Germania*, Il Saggiatore, 1995.

Fest Joachim, *Hitler*, Harcourt Brace & Co, 1992.

Fulbrook Mary, *The Divided Nation: A History of Germany, 1918–1990*, Oxford University Press, 1992.

Goebbels Joseph, *Goebbels Diaries 1942–1943*, Greenwood, reprint, 1970.

Janik Allen, Toulmin Stephen, *Wittgenstein's Vienna*, Ivan R. Dee Inc., 1996.

Laqueur Walter, *Weimar: a cultural history: 1918–1933*, Weidenfeld and Nicholson Ltd., 1973.

Liddell Hart B.H., *History of the Second World War*, Da Capo Press, 1999.

Mosse George, *The Crisis of German Ideology: Intellectual Origins of the Third Reich*, Howard Fertig, Inc., 1997.

Ricciotti Lazzero, *Gli Schiavi di Hitler*, Mondadori, 1996.

Sereny Gitta, *Albert Speer: His Battle with Truth*, Vintage Books, 1996.

Shirer William L., *The Rise and Fall of the Third Reich*, Buccaneer Books, 1991.

Speer Albert, *Inside the Third Reich*, Simon & Schuster, 1997.

Taylor Telford, *The Anatomy of the Nuremberg Trials: A personal Memoir*, Little Brown & Co., 1993.

To better understand the socio-political climate of the United States in the Fifties:

Halberstamm David, *The Fifties*, Ballantine Books, 1994.

These 800 pages contain rigorous analyses of everything that happened in the period. The author won the Pulitzer Prize.

To augment the history of the Beetle and other VW vehicles:

Battazi Marco, *Volkswagen Maggiolino*, G. Nada Editore, 1989.

Buhrnam Colin, *Classic Volkswagen: Colour Classics*, Osprey UK, 1996.

Etzold Hans-Rudiger, *The Beetle: the Chronicles of the People's Car: Production & Evolution, Facts & Figures*, Haynes Publications, 1997.

Meredith Laurence, *The Original VW Beetle*, Motorbooks International, 1994.

Pasi Alessandro, *Il Maggiolino*, Marsilio, 1996.

Pasini Stefano, *Porsche 356*, Automobilia Classic, 1993.

Prew Clive, *VW Beetle*, Bison Group, 1990.

Shuler Terry, *The Origin & Evolution of the VW Beetle*, Automobile Quarterly Books, 1985.

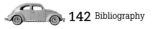

Photo Credits

With great appreciation to everyone
who helped contribute photographs
for this book:

Volkswagen AG

Agenzia AP

Architectural Digest

Auto Oggi Archive

Centro Documentazione AME, Milan

Mario De Biasi

Manuel Del Grande, Milan

Elliott Erwit

Peter Keetman

Thomas Maccabelli

Alessandro Pasi

Alberto Pejrano

Photo Frank Camuzat, Paris

Photo Kiki

Keith Seume, GB

R.K. Smith, USA

S. Szantai, USA

In addition, the publisher thanks
Bburago SpA, Burago Molgora, Milan
for the loan of model cars.

The publisher is available to parties
holding rights to images which may
not have been identified.